Haunted Kentucky
Tales of a Conduit

Haunted Kentucky

Tales of a Conduit

Terri Grimes

DM Publications

Haunted Kentucky
Tales of a Conduit

Copyright 2014 by Terri Grimes
All rights reserved

No part of this publication may be reproduced or transmitted in any form or by any means, electronic or mechanical, including photo-copy, recording or any information storage and retrieval system, without permission in writing. The exception being in the case of brief quotations embodied in articles and reviews. For detailed information contact the author.

Printed in The United States of America

www.terrigrimes.com

Copyright © 2014 Terri Grimes

All rights reserved.

ISBN-10: 149596678X
ISBN-13: 978-1495966781

DEDICATION

Dedicated to those who have passed on before us, especially my Mother-in-Law, Marion Grimes who showed me a glimpse of Heaven.

PROLOGUE
i

Chapter One
CENTRAL STATE ASYLUM
1

Chapter Two
SAUERKRAUT CAVE
5

Chapter Three
CEMETERIES OF CENTRAL STATE ASYLUM
13

Chapter Four
CONFEDERATE CEMETERY
19

Chapter Five
CONRAD CALDWELL HOUSE
27

Chapter Six
BENJAMIN HEAD HOUSE
33

Chapter Seven
NUNNLEA HOUSE
39

Chapter Eight
GERMAN REFORMED CEMETERY
47

Chapter Nine
MIDDLETOWN TOY MUSEUM
53

Chapter Ten
MIDDLETOWN HISTORIC CEMETERY
61

Chapter Eleven
LONG RUN CEMETERY
67

Chapter Twelve
BUFFALO TRACE
73

Chapter Thirteen
MT EDEN CEMETERY
77

Chapter Fourteen
OCTAGON HALL
83

Chapter Fifteen
BOONE TAVERN
89

Chapter Sixteen
HAYSWOOD HOSPITAL
95

Chapter Seventeen
FARMINGTON
99

Chapter Eighteen
LOCUST GROVE
103

Chapter Nineteen
ASHLAND
107

Chapter Twenty
WHEN SPIRITS FOLLOW YOU HOME
111

Chapter Twenty-One
ORBS
117

Chapter Twenty-Two
ELECTRONIC VOICE PHENOMENON
121

Chapter Twenty-Three
PARANORMAL TERMINOLOGY
125

Chapter Twenty-Four
HAUNTED LOCATIONS
131

PROLOGUE

When my husband and I first moved to Louisville Kentucky in July 2009 I was writing the first in a series of books about a ghost investigator who falls in love with a demon hunter. Although admittedly I didn't start out with the intention of becoming a ghost hunter, what better way to learn about ghost hunting than by becoming one myself.

Even before we finished unpacking I'd started my paranormal journey by visiting some of the local hotspots everyone claimed were off the charts with unexplained activity. I wanted to get a true feel for what a haunted location felt like, so I could make my novel more believable. As I visited these spots an amazing thing happened, I started having unique paranormal experiences at each and every haunted property.

My next step was to interview the local paranormal groups. What equipment do you use most often? Have you ever been attacked by a spirit? How can you remove a demon from a location? Throughout that process I kept hearing, "There's an informative ghost hunting class at the University of Louisville." So many people mentioned the class to me that I began to think there must be something to it. When the Fall semester came around, I signed up for the class. It was there I met Carrie, the class instructor and founder of Kentucky Paranormal Research. Through her I learned that my paranormal experiences and the wealth of evidence I was experiencing in my new home state was far from normal.

That first night when I walked into the classroom and introduced myself, I got the impression Carrie had heard, "I'm a ghost magnet," more than once. But when I brought in some of the evidence I'd captured I could sense her perception of me changing. By the time we'd been on a couple of ghost hunting expeditions together she'd changed my terminology of 'ghost magnet' to 'conduit.'

As the class progressed I learned that other people don't normally have the quality and quantity of paranormal experiences that I'd been having. I also discovered that Kentucky sits on a bed of limestone, which many experts claim aids spirits in coming through. Could that be the reason I was having such ease in communicating with the other side?

I invited Carrie to meet me for lunch. Over chicken salad sandwiches and tomato basil soup I learned I was likely a combination of the perfect storm once I'd moved to Kentucky. Not only was the limestone allowing the paranormal to be more evident, but years earlier I'd had two near death experiences where I'd been in the light and as Carrie explained, that made the veil between life and death much thinner for me.

A year after our conversation, after taking another walk in the light—this time during open-heart surgery—the veil became almost nonexistent to the point where I was hearing disembodied voices and seeing spirits as well. I didn't even have to be in a haunted location to experience the paranormal. It was happening everywhere I went after the open-heart surgery, even in my own home.

After a week at home I had a significant setback, causing me to return to the hospital for further treatment which would save my life. I took my voice recorder with me and conducted several EVP sessions alone in my hospital room at 3:00 o'clock in the morning. What I captured amazed me.

"Who are you?" I asked in one session.

"I'm a patient just like you," a young female replied.

The highlight was the night I caught a familiar voice. It was that of my beloved and very deceased grandmother. To know that she was with me—albeit in spirit—to help me through the rough times in my life, meant the world to me.

I spoke with other people who'd gone through heart valve replacement and learned that many of them had similar memories of being in the light while their heart was stopped during the operation. Most had experienced paranormal occurrences after the surgery as well. My heart surgeon told me this was normal and could cease after six months, or a year, or possibly continue for the rest of my life.

It's been two years since my open-heart surgery and spirits still flock to me like moths to a flame.

1

CENTRAL STATE ASYLUM

Located in the eastern part of Louisville Kentucky is a 550-acre property now known as E.P. Tom Sawyer Park. The grounds were originally deeded to Isaac Hite in 1784 for his service in the Virginia Militia. He titled his newly acquired property, "Cave Spring Plantation." Murdered by Indians at 41 years of age, Isaac was the first to meet with an untimely death on the grounds.

The Hite family would remain on the land until 1869 when the property was sold and the "Home for Juvenile Delinquents at Lakeland" was built.

By 1873 the facility was converted into the state's fourth lunatic asylum and renamed "Central Kentucky Lunatic Asylum." In 1887 the name was changed again to "Lakeland Asylum." By the early 1900's, the official name reverted to "Central Kentucky Asylum for the Insane." Later and lastly it became known as "Central State Hospital."

In 1986, when Central State's new facility was completed on nearby LaGrange Road, the property was given to the State Parks Department and E.P. Tom Sawyer Park was built. The original facility and several outbuildings would stand empty until the mid 1990's when they were demolished.

Today most people think all that remains of the asylum are a couple of outbuildings. That is far from true. The eastern edge of the park, next to a ridge where the old asylum used to stand, is known as shelter three. In the center of the ridge stands a plaque imprinted with a panoramic picture of the mental institution in its heyday. What the general public doesn't know is that when they stand on the ridge, they're actually standing on top of the asylum.

Only the top stories of the structure were razed. Full demolition would have been in the millions. It was more cost effective to leave the basement and flooring of the first floor. Fill dirt was dumped over the remains of the large building, creating a man made ridge. Often in a heavy rain, objects wash up to the surface. Pottery, pieces of metal bed frames, you name it. I was to experience things popping up out of the ground for myself when I investigated the ridge and discovered a piece of the buildings rebar poking out of the ground.

When I found out that the base of Central State's massive building still remained under the earth, I knew why I'd captured some of my clearest EVP's on top of that ridge. It was obvious to me that the structure was retaining and heightening the paranormal activity. People were still stuck in its walls, despite them being underground.

Every path you walk on in Tom Sawyer Park seems to hold a memory of days gone by. Evident by the cries for help heard in disembodied voices or caught in EVPs, the memories these acres hold aren't always pleasant ones and far too often they seep into the fabric of the living.

I placed one hand on the rebar and began my EVP session. I often find that if I touch something associated with the spirits, such as a headstone or even a wall of the building they lived in, I have better success communicating with them.

"Does anyone need help?"

A woman's voice spoke with an urgent tone in my voice recorder. "Can I please go home?"

Not knowing I'd caught a Class-A EVP, I continued the session, coaxing the spirits to speak and tell me their story. At that point a child took me up on my offer and began to talk. The young boy's voice said simply, "Dear God, help me."

~ * ~

There are many trails throughout the park. One section of trails that many comment on is near where the asylum stood. Reports of paranormal occurrences on these trails are numerous. This is the area of the property where the patients were taken on daily therapeutic walks. Nowadays this section of pathways is known as "the crazy loop."

As I walked these trails, I sensed I wasn't alone. Every several feet I would stop and listen for accompanying footsteps, sometimes hearing them. The hair stood up on the back of my neck and a chill ran up the length of my spine. I stopped and looked upward. As I observed a small object flying through the sky, seemingly appearing out of thin air, I caught a class A evp of a male voice on my recorder saying, "Get out!" Then the object fell from the sky, landing an inch from my foot.

Examining the object, I could see it was a chunk of brick. More importantly it was a chunk from the homemade bricks found in the Sauerkraut Cave. I stood in shock, reality taking time to sink in. One week prior, I'd stood in the cave, taunting the male presence. Was this chunk of brick retaliation or a warning? Either way, I wasn't about to stand around to find out and quickly made my way back to my vehicle.

Sitting in my van, I recounted the experience in my voice recorder while it was still fresh in my mind. A futile gesture because there was no way I'd soon forget it. As I struggled to regain my composure, I noticed the air held a heavy, thickness. Despite the warm day, it was getting considerably colder in the small confines of my van. I had company.

"Who is in here with me?"

"I'm behind you," a male voice said.

"Do you need help crossing over into the light?"

The male responded, "Have you considered we're where we belong?"

No, I'd never considered earthbound spirits to be where they belonged. I'd had a glimpse of Heaven three times and I couldn't imagine anyone wanting to be anywhere but in the light. Could it be that I was wrong in wanting all the spirits to go into the light as I had? The concept was giving the term 'free will' a whole new meaning to me.

2

SAUERKRAUT CAVE

Hidden in the woods of Tom Sawyer Park is a cave that many call the Springhouse. During the period when the Isaac Hite family occupied the property in the 1780's, they referred to the natural structure as Sauerkraut Cave after the numerous stoneware vats of sauerkraut they stored there to cure. The cave would become such an integral part of their lives that they named their home Cave Springs Plantation. It's known that there was even a mill built adjacent to the cave, which used the natural force of the underground spring running under the cave to power the operation. On early maps the location is referred to as Hite's Mill.

Comprised of two rooms with earthen ceiling and floors, the back room has an opening which tunnels under the park property, all the way past Hurstbourne Parkway and to the Ohio River. To fortify the cave, the Hite family lined the walls with handmade bricks, and fashioned doors for the entrance. They took advantage of the natural aqueduct that ran under the cave, enhancing it by channeling a stream inside the cave in order to use it as a coolant, keeping the chambers chilled even on the hottest summer days. That made the cave a perfect spot to store sauerkraut, milk, butter, and any number of items that needed to be kept cool back in the days before refrigeration.

Some claim that during the years that Lakeland aka Central State Asylum held the property in the later 1800's and early to mid 1900's, Sauerkraut Cave was also used to store dead bodies until they could be buried in one of the two cemeteries on the property. Regardless of its use, all who visit agree on one thing—it's creepy.

It's known that there were many occurrences of rape at the asylum. The culprits were sometimes patients, but more often the caregivers. When a female would become pregnant, male employees would take her in the cave and perform an abortion. They weren't doctors, so frequently the female would die from the experience. It's only natural that the walls of the cave would be imprinted with the horrors that occurred in its confines.

Through EVPs I learned of another horror that occurred in the cave. A male patient, who was confined to the asylum for "not being able to keep his hands to himself," lured a young boy into the Springhouse and murdered him. The presence of the murderer lurks in the back room of the cave, bragging through evp about his deeds.

Orbs often appear in pictures people take of the back of the cave. Sometimes these orbs will have a face imprinted in the center. Several people, myself included, have seen a brief glimpse against the back wall, of a man who appears to be from the late 1800's or early 1900's. I would come to know that man on a personal level.

I returned to the Springhouse on a chilly March morning. Two friends from Delaware—George and Allen—were spending their Spring vacation with us and were anxious to go on a ghost hunt. I had just the places for them.

When we arrived at Sauerkraut Cave and I stepped into the back room I could feel my heart rate accelerate. Every hair on the back of my neck and arms stood straight up. I closed my eyes and reached out with the rest of my senses to whatever beings shared the small space with me. I shivered when I felt a cool breath blow past my right ear. My lips curved into a smile as I opened my eyes. Let the games begin.

"Who is with us today?" I asked.

I could see George and Allen quietly watching me as they stood barely in the entrance of the cave. I motioned for them to come deeper in the springhouse and join me in the second room. At first they both shook their head, declining the invitation, but several minutes later their curiosity outnumbered their fear and they joined me in the back room.

Through the ever-present sound of water trickling over the stones in the brick lined cistern that ran the length of the left side of the Springhouse, back into areas far too small for us to explore, we could hear voices. We couldn't make out all of the words, but all three of us were certain the voices were discussing us.

Meandering back into the front of the cave, near the entrance, Allen explored a nook hidden by the overflowing pile of bricks dumped unceremoniously at the right side of the front cave.

George and I heard a startled yelp and raced over to see what the commotion was. Allen stood, slack jawed. "I swear I just saw a man standing next to me in this corner by the bricks."

I pulled out my IR Temperature gun and was amazed to find the temperature 41 degrees in that spot, considerably colder than the rest of the cave. Immediately I snapped a picture, capturing a thick mist that appeared to form a head and face, clearly looking at us.

George stood next to Allen with his voice recorder and they both urged the entity to communicate with them through the device.

"Can you tell me how you died?" George asked.

Later at home we all shivered when we reviewed George's EVP's and heard a spirit reply, "I had the water end my life. Would you like to join me?"

I had to hand it to George and Allen; although the places I took them were the first formal ghost hunting experiences they'd had, they were able to hang with me, experience for experience, going in places and situations many seasoned investigators would hesitate to go in.

~ * ~

It was 103 degrees when I took two young ladies—Jasmine and Kiley—to Tom Sawyer on a July morning in 2012. As I'd come to count on, the cave was uncomfortably cold, despite the heat wave Louisville was enduring. It hadn't rained in weeks and the entire state of Kentucky was dry and brittle. As we went in the cave that day, it was no surprise to see the cave floor dusty. Gone was the wet slippery mud we'd experienced when I'd gone in the caves earlier in the spring.

We caught our first EVP shortly after entering the first room of the cave. I asked, "Does anyone want to communicate with us?"

A male voice responded on my voice recorder, "Over here." Immediately afterwards a woman added, "Stay with us."

Our EVP session was cut short when a voice whispered close to Jasmine's ear, causing her to run from the cave. She couldn't make out what the voice said, but it was a male voice and most definitely creepy. Meanwhile I started walking from the first room to the back of the cave, but before I could step over the brick threshold between the two rooms I suddenly began to slip and slide like I was standing on wet, slimy mud. I had great difficulty keeping myself upright. At the time it confused me because the dirt floor of the cave was dry and dusty. Things became clearer when I reviewed the EVP's I'd caught and heard the negative male entity from the back of the cave say, "I grabbed her feet." That explained why every time I attempted to move from the spot it felt like my feet were going to go out from under me. Later, when Jasmine and Kiley came back in the cave to help me, they caught an EVP of the same male saying, "Did your foot slip Terri? Did you like it?"

Jasmine and Kiley later told me they'd seen a mist following me around in the cave that morning. And after reviewing the few pictures I'd taken and seeing orbs in most of them. I had to agree, it was a place where extreme caution needed to be taken.

I returned to the cave two months later on a mild October night. My friend Carrie had brought her ghost hunting class to the park and asked me to give them a tour of the cave, leading them through a dowsing rod and EVP session.

Although the cave had it's usual creepy vibe, activity was quiet, initially. When we had significant responses to our dowsing rod session you could feel the students excitement growing. Then I made serious mistake. I called on the negative entity residing in the back of the cave. I point-blank asked him, "Did you hurt a young boy in this cave?"

I heard a low rumble of laughter, followed by several four-letter words.

The student standing next to me gasped in fright. My vision panned to the area she was staring. There, lounging against the wall of the cave was a transparent male figure. A figure I would later come to know well, after our visit to the cemetery located on the grounds of the park.

Later that night, after the students left and only Carrie and I remained in the parking lot, I felt an urge to take a picture of my empty vehicle. Moments later, as I started driving home I felt an overwhelming sensation of not being alone in the SUV. So much so, that I called Carrie on my cell and had her follow me home, remaining on the phone with me the entire time.

As I reviewed the pictures that night, I realized I was right, I hadn't been alone on the ride home. For there, right behind the wheel of my SUV, was the negative entity from the cave.

Not only did the negative spirit follow me home, he stayed for almost a week. I would feel the back of my hair being tugged as I sat on the couch watching television. Occasionally my husband and I would hear faint knocking sounds or footsteps. But the night I took a picture of the Christmas village scene I'd just set up in my china cupboard I knew it was time to force my unwelcome visitor to leave, because there, in the side glass door of the hutch was the entity's face.

    I burned white sage and wafting the smoke in every corner of my home, said positive affirmations allowing only positive energies remain. With that, the negative presence left my home and hasn't returned.

3
CEMETERIES OF CENTRAL STATE ASYLUM

In addition to allegations of patient abuse, after an extensive investigation the Kentucky Grand Jury ruled in 1943 that Central State was unfairly committing and imprisoning people who were not mentally ill.

Some of the atrocities discovered were overcrowding, mental and physical abuse. It was learned that they used insulin therapy, forced freezing cold showers, lobotomies and electroshocks as treatments. Central State was far from the happy place they tried to portray it as.

The lack of compassion and ill treatment didn't end with death as often they were dumped unceremoniously in one of several unmarked trenches in the graveyards. Numerous deaths went unreported and uninvestigated. Many of the records kept were eventually lost. It's unknown exactly how many patients are buried on the hospital grounds, but it's estimated to be upwards of 5,000. I've only been able to track down the names of 443 patients buried on the grounds. Is it any wonder they're not at rest?

Today the four gravestones that remain are piled haphazardly the tree in the center of the large graveyard. Only two of the four have readable names with the oldest having a death date of 1895. However, it's known that the smallest of the two graveyards originated prior to the 1880's.

Over the years human bones frequently came to the surface during heavy rains or were washed into the creek. Headstones have been found in the creek bed as well. You can see where some of the graves once were by the prominent sinkholes dotting the landscape. The people interred here seem to be aware of the lack of respect they've been given, and have no problem in letting the living know of their pain as I was soon to discover.

The first time I explored the larger of the two graveyards was in 2010 on a chilly evening in mid November. Fellow ghost hunters, Carrie and Tony, along with my friend and neighbor, Pat and myself had just finished an investigation of the Springhouse. Although it was nearing 9:00 o'clock, the brilliance of the full moon made it almost unnecessary to use our flashlights. There was a distinct heaviness in the air as we approached the graveyard. If you closed your eyes you could feel the caresses of the dead as they surrounded us.

This was the first time any of us had been in the graveyard area of Tom Sawyer Park and we were dismayed to see that the metal gate connecting the wooden fence surrounding the large graveyard was locked with a heavy metal chain and padlock. As I stood there in front of the locked gate I said to my companions, "I'm going to climb the fence. I hope I don't get caught." Pat just shook her head and grinned, not saying a word. She knew me well and was used to my spontaneous behavior. Upon review of my digital voice recording you can clearly hear a whispery male voice respond, "Go ahead."

After I risked life and limb to climb over the rickety wooden structure, I had to laugh. Because everyone else walked through the open space, three feet away from the gate, where a large section of fence was missing. So much for being spontaneous.

Once inside the graveyard we all began taking pictures.

"Could you appear in front of my camera?" I asked. I was delighted to see bright orbs appearing in my pictures on the LCD screen of my camera.

"Thank you, I appreciate your cooperation. Who is here with us?"

My voice recorder caught a young male voice, "Roy. My name is Roy."

Not realizing I'd just caught an EVP in response to my question, I said to Carrie, "I feel like we're not alone."

Before she had a chance to answer an eerie female voice on my recorder said, "I'm here. Look down lower."

I'm always amazed to hear spirits responding to conversations I have with other investigators. So many times I've heard spirits say things that make it obvious they've been eavesdropping as we converse.

While everyone went to the far end of the property near the tree line, I remained in the center of the graveyard, by the tree that had the four headstones surrounding it. Although I wasn't seeing apparitions or hearing disembodied voices, by the raised hair on my arms and the tingly feeling on the back of my neck I knew a spirit was close by.

"Do you know the cave area? Maybe you know it as the springhouse? Could you tell me, is there a bad person there?"

I captured an EVP of a male responding, "There is no good there."

I continued with my line of questioning. "Should I stay away from there?" The same male voice continued to warn me. "There is nothing there for you but evil. Stay away."

The next day, after reviewing the EVPs I'd caught, it chilled me to the bone hearing this young man warn me about the Springhouse. Although the general rule is that you should never investigate a haunted location alone, I'd often foolishly ignored that advice. Hearing the spirit's warning, I vowed never to go to the cave alone again. But I didn't make a vow about the graveyard. After what happened during my next visit maybe I should have.

~ * ~

It was 9:00 o'clock on a February morning when I returned to the graveyard. I could see my breath in the air, but the brilliance of the sun and lack of breeze made it seem much warmer than it was.

Walking to the center of the graveyard, I turned my voice recorder on, laying it atop the gravestone labeled, "Aunt Florence." The unnatural silence to the air that morning was unnerving. Although I was the only one there it felt like hundreds of pairs of eyes were watching me. The feeling was so intense, I started rapidly snapping pictures as I slowly turned in a complete circle. Usually that practice turns up phenomenal paranormal evidence. This time was no exception. Later, reviewing the pictures I saw a dark shadow in the form of a person, peeking out from behind a tree, watching me. It wore what a hat which seemed to be a style from many years ago. You could see right through the figure.

Then I said, "If there is anyone here with me today, could you give me a sign of your presence?" How does the parable go; be careful what you ask for because you might get it?

Several things happened in rapid succession. First I caught a Class-A EVP of a male saying, "Can't tell." Less than sixty seconds later a train from the nearby tracks in Anchorage blew its whistle. Then a police siren wailed as the car zoomed down a distant road. I mumbled, more to myself then anyone else, "Not that I can hear you over the sound of the train and siren. You're going to have to speak pretty loud for me to hear you over all this noise."

The words had barely escaped my lips when suddenly I heard the sound of someone screaming loudly. I couldn't believe what I was hearing. My initial thought was that I was mistaking the sound of a dog howling for a woman's screams. But then another voice joined the woman, both of them screaming in unison and then another voice and another.

"What the heck?" I said, my jaw hanging agape. I stood in the center of the cemetery in shock as the sound of many people screaming and pleading for help resonated around me. I was hearing the disembodied voices of the dead. To me it sounded like it was a full moon and all the crazies had escaped from the lunatic asylum. To this day it remains the most powerful paranormal experience I've ever had. I could hear distinct voices screaming, "Help me" and "No." I could feel their agony as they screamed in pain and despair.

After a full two minutes, standing alone in the middle of the screams, I did what any sane person would do. I turned and ran toward the gate. Midway between where I had been standing in the center of the cemetery and the gate, I fell in an open hole. I didn't know it at the time, but at the moment I fell in the hole—an open grave—I caught an angry female voice on my voice recorder, snapping, "Get off me." When I stepped on the other side of the gate, the screams stopped. Instantly. I stood there wondering if I had imagined the entire episode. Warily I ventured back through the open gate, taking two steps into the cemetery. As soon as I did the screams began again. This time when I ran out of the cemetery I kept on going.

It was two days before I could summon the courage to listen to my recording session. Part of me hoped I didn't catch what I thought I'd heard, while the investigator part of me lusted after the experience. It was all there though. The train whistle, the police siren and each and every disembodied scream. I could even make out the specific words I'd heard that day such as, "No, save me" and "Help me." Even to this day, cold chills run up my spine when I listen to the EVP I caught that morning.

To hear disembodied voices at 9:30 on a bright sunny morning and to capture the entire experience on audio was the holy grail.

Holy grail or not, it was a long time before I went back. When I did go back, it was with a film crew. I had filmed the first portion of "My Ghost Story Caught on Camera," in Los Angeles California. They wanted to film the reenactment segment on location. That's how I came to be standing in the center of the graveyard at 10 o'clock at night in nine degree weather.

As we filmed that night. I knew the spirits were curious, wondering what we were doing. Without hesitation I told them our purpose and invited them to watch the process. The director urged me to take pictures as if I were on an actual paranormal investigation, as the cameraman filmed me. I snapped picture after picture, in addition to using my digital voice recorder.

The next day, when I downloaded the pictures I'd taken that night, I was amazed at the number of spirits I'd captured in the trees.

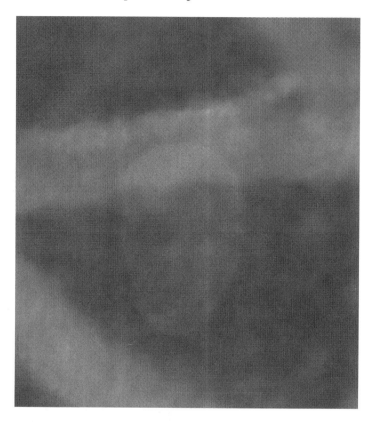

One of the faces among the bare branches was familiar to me. The face was the same one I'd seen in the cave, in my SUV and even in my home—my nemesis—the negative male entity.

The chilling part was when I listened to the EVPs. The male entity was urging the other spirits to attack the camera man, ordering, "Kick him, punch him, hurt him." Each instruction of harm coincided with the camera man tripping, getting a severe stomach pain for several minutes and having his equipment fall over. Chilling, indeed.

CONFEDERATE CEMETERY

Listed on the National Register of Historic Places, the Confederate Cemetery is located near the site of the old Kentucky Confederate Home in

Pewee Valley. This is the only cemetery for Confederate veterans, 313 in total, which is an official state burying ground in Kentucky.

Erected near the front of cemetery is the Confederate Memorial monument. The monument is unique for Kentucky's Civil War monuments in that it is built of zinc, whereas most are made of marble or limestone.

While the cemetery was organized in the spring of 1872 and plants placed to beautify the area, it wasn't until 1902, when the Kentucky state assembly unanimously approved the building of a veteran's home specifically for Confederate veterans of the American Civil War by the cemetery, that the cemetery was given it's current name. It was also at that time that the cemetery was divided into three parts; one for Confederate veterans, one for whites and one for blacks.

Instrumental in getting approval the Confederate Home and later the burial space was former Confederate officer Bennett H. Young. He had long desired such a facility as he saw that many former Confederate veterans were no longer able to take care of themselves, either financially or physically.

In the years the Confederate Home was an active veterans facility, it provided a hospital, nursing care, food, entertainment, and religious services for up to 350 veterans at a time, providing a home for 700 former Confederate soldiers throughout its years of operation. The requirements to be a resident of the home was to not only be a former Confederate soldier, but to have been a resident of Kentucky for the past six months, be mentally stable, and to have no problems with alcoholism. Many of the veterans once served under John Hunt Morgan, Lee Jackson and the fourth Kentucky Infantry, "Orphan Brigade."

When it closed in 1934, the five remaining men were transferred to the nearby Pewee Valley Sanatorium. All that remains of the Home is its main gate, which serves as the entrance arch for the Confederate Cemetery.

My first visit to the Confederate Cemetery was on an overly warm Sunday afternoon in August 2010. It was too hot to do much of anything that weekend other than hunker down indoors in air-conditioned comfort. By Sunday I was going stir-crazy from sitting inside.

"What about a long drive in the country and then a casual dinner out?" my husband offered.

I eagerly accepted his idea. Any plan that included my not having to cook was a good one as far as I was concerned. So that's how we ended up in the car driving on Route 146 that day. We'd been living in Louisville for only a year, having moved here from Indianapolis, so we enjoyed exploring the beautiful state of Kentucky.

Passing through a small area called Peewee Valley, we drove at a sedate pace to get a good look at the gorgeous architecture of the stately homes. Many looked to be more than 100 years old. As we neared Maple Street we saw a sign for the Confederate Cemetery. Greg and I looked at each other for a split second before simultaneously nodding our heads in agreement. Being big Civil War buffs, we were always up for a trek involving any aspect of that era. The fact that it was a cemetery made it all the more attractive to me. It was the best of both worlds. We'd both get a dose of Civil War history and I'd get the added bonus of doing some paranormal investigating. I always carry my camera and digital voice recorder with me, just for this very purpose.

The arched sign over the entrance as we drove in the cemetery gave me my first tingle of excitement. It read, "Kentucky Confederate Home, Dedicated October 23, 1902." I was anxious to park in the spacious parking lot so I could get out and roam among the graves.

Reading the different Units on the headstones, I turned to Greg. "Which Calvary Unit did John Hunt Morgan ride in?"

"I think it was the First Kentucky Calvary, or maybe it was the Second."

Unbeknownst to us a male spirit was listening to our conversation and spoke in my voice recorder, "Second. He was in the Second Calvary."

Later, when I was reviewing the EVP, I looked it up online and sure enough John Hunt Morgan rode in the Second Kentucky Calvary.

Another interesting EVP I caught that day occurred just a minute later when the same male voice said, "Morgan was a punk." He was obviously not a fan of John Hunt Morgan.

I laid my digital voice recorder on one of the confederate soldier's headstones. That's a practice I often do in a cemetery. It usually gets me positive results and starts a dialogue with the graves inhabitant. This time it merely served to make the spirit angry. When I played the EVP session back I could clearly hear an irritated, older sounding male voice bark, "Damn-it, get that thing off my head!"

That same afternoon I had another spirit take offense to me. If you know anything about Kentucky, you know that lawn gnats and mosquitoes are fond of warm Summer afternoons. That's how I found myself swatting at the buzzing pests circling my head, to the point that I was becoming beyond frustrated. "Cut it out you bloody scallywag!" I shouted at one particularly persistent insect.

Upon playback I heard another angry male voice demand, "Who are you calling a scallywag?"

Moral of the story; I should be more careful about what I say in a graveyard.

~ * ~

I didn't make it back to the Confederate Graveyard until that December, although it had been in the back of my mind frequently. I was feeling a pull to the peaceful spot. In December I found out just how peaceful it truly was.

My husband and I absolutely adore BBQ. It could be from the fact that we used to have our own competition BBQ team or more likely from the fact that we just love to eat. One, or both, of those loves urges us to Kentucky's best BBQ, Jucy's. The Confederate Cemetery is conveniently located less than ¼ mile from Jucy's on Maple Road. So that night, after stuffing our bellies full of beef brisket and smoky pork ribs, I had the brilliant idea to make a night time trek to the cemetery.

I've been to several other cemeteries at night, and while they all have a distinct air of activity once the sun goes now, I've never felt a malevolence or uneasiness. This night was different. From the moment we drove through the gates both Greg and I felt that we were intruding and unwelcome.

Greg opted to stay in the car. A shame really, because you couldn't get a true sense of appreciation for how active this place was that night without standing in the midst of it. Unknowingly Greg was getting a true sense for the amount of activity inside our SUV.

Exiting the vehicle, I stood for a few moments at the edge of the neatly lined confederate headstones. As I perused the dark graveyard my voice recorder picked up a male voice demanding, "Why do you come now?"

The cemetery was as dark as pitch and I could sense things moving around in the darkness. I didn't feel alone. I saw a familiar shape moving among the trees about the height of where a flag might be. I couldn't remember if there was a flag in the cemetery or not so I said aloud to the spirits, "Is there a flag up there?" I caught an EVP of a male voice whispering, "What's up there? What's she looking at?" A second male voice whispered, "A flag I think. Is there a flag?"

About a minute later I was abruptly aware of a tall, dark, solid mass standing about 3 inches to the left side of me. The mass was the shape and height of an adult.

I jumped and gasped. It had startled me because it wasn't something I was expecting. Although no longer visible, I apologized to the spirit for my reaction.

There was a foreboding in the air and I left shortly thereafter. Instinctually I knew we weren't supposed to be there and the spirits wanted me to leave. On my way back to our vehicle, I took a picture of my SUV. It's not something I normally do, but that night I felt led to do it. Once back in the car I let my voice recorder continue recording until we were off of the property and back on Route 146.

At home reviewing the EVP's I'd captured, a shiver ran up my spine when I got to the point in my audio where the dark, human shaped mass had stood next to me. At that exact moment I'd caught an EVP of a man saying close to the microphone, "Hi." As excited as I was to capture the Class-A EVP, I had no idea my night was about to get even better.

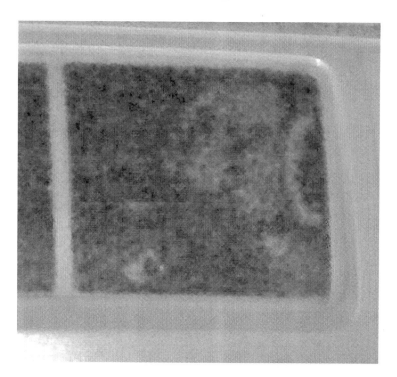

I downloaded the pictures off my trusty Nikon digital, onto my laptop. I carefully perused each high-resolution picture, one by one. An orb here or an orb there was about all I caught. Then I saw the last picture I'd taken that night; the random shot of our SUV. I froze. For there, in the middle seat of my our Nissan Pathfinder was a transparent dog, looking out of the window. He looked like a Beagle. And just above him, slightly to the right, was another dog—a larger dog and one I knew well. For the larger dog was unmistakably our twelve year old, very much deceased, family pet. Moose died in March 2008 of anal sac carcinoma—cancer. Greg and I still get teary eyed when we think of Moose. We miss him so much. As Greg has often said, we've almost cried more tears over that dog than if one of our children had died. And truly, isn't the family dog one of the children? He was certainly an important and vital member of our family. And he is still with us, even in death.

As for the beagle, I can't really say who that might be. Moose is the only pet we've ever had, even to this day. However, when we lived in Indianapolis, our neighbor had several beagles. One was close in age to our Moose and would run the length of the bordering fence with him every day. He died two years after Moose. Could they be reunited in death to the point of taking a ride together in our SUV? I guess we won't know until we cross the shimmering veil ourselves.

I enlarged the picture and poured over it inch by inch, seeing things I'd missed at first glance. Above the vehicle is a bright orb. And in the far back cargo area—an area where my husband had folded the seats down and had nothing in—was another dog, crouched near the back window.

That wouldn't be the only time I was to capture Moose's image in our SUV. To this day, when I take a nighttime picture of that SUV when on an investigation, I frequently have his image appear in the back seat.

But then, as I looked at that picture, I felt excitement coursing through my veins. If I could get EVP's from our hitchhikers it would be pretty darned perfect. I put my headphones on and fast forwarded to the last few minutes of the recording, when we were leaving the cemetery. I could hear the sound of the car door open and then close as I got back into the vehicle.

"Did you get what you came for?"

"More than I bargained for," I heard myself replying to my husband, thinking back to solid black shape that stood next to me in the graveyard.

Suddenly a male voice hissed in the voice recorder, "Get out. Get your autobus out of my house!"

Still listening to the recording I heard Greg and I chatting as he turned the key and shifted into drive. As I finished detailing experiences in the graveyard to him, a male voice whispers, "Go on and follow her." And then a different male voice says, "Come on down here and help me."

It's a good thing our SUV seats seven because between the ghost dogs and the numerous Confederate soldiers that were hitching a ride with us that night, we were full up.

5

CONRAD CALDWELL HOUSE

Some say that the recipe for a haunted location is an act of violence or great tragedy. I disagree. Sure, I admit it's probable that trauma may cause a person to hang around longer than they should. But I'd go a step further and say that love can keep a person grounded just as easily. It could be love for another person who hasn't yet passed to the other side or love for a location.

Take for instance the Conrad Caldwell mansion on the historic St. James Square. Over the years the stately home has been so well loved, that several of the occupants still reside there, years after their death. After touring the home and later serving as a docent during their Christmas open house, I can see why.

Originally built by Theophile Conrad, the mansion, located in what's now known as Old Town Louisville, was completed in 1894 for a grand total of seventy-five thousand dollars, an extravagant amount of money at the time. Making his fortune in leathers and furs as the owner and operator of Conrad Tanning Company, Theophile Conrad was able to hire such greats as famed architects Arthur Loomis and Charles Clarke. They would use only the finest materials and latest innovations of the time in creating this magnificent home. People referred to the estate as Conrad Castle or Conrad's Folly. Today the Conrad-Caldwell House is considered the best residential example of Loomis' Richardsonian Romanesque style.

Following Mr. Conrad's death in 1905, his wife, Maria, sold the home for fifty thousand dollars to family friends William and Elaine Caldwell.

Owner of the Caldwell Tank Company, William Caldwell was an astute engineer and businessman. He and his wife Elaine, with their children, Grace and Walter would make the mansion their home for thirty-five years.

After Mr. Caldwell's death in 1938, the mansion was deeded to a local woman who ran it as a boarding house until 1947, at which time the Presbyterian Church purchased the home. Renaming the mansion, The Rose Anna Hughes Home for Widows, it was used as a retirement home for almost forty years.

In 1987 the home was purchased by a local trust and restored, becoming the beautiful historic mansion that we enjoy today. Fortunately the Caldwell family retained many of the lovely furnishings and personal items that adorned the home during William and Maria's occupancy, which they generously donated to the trust. With the addition of the items the Conrad family donated, the mansion is fully restored in circa 1908.

Both William Caldwell and his daughter Grace had an abiding affection for the stately home, one that wouldn't end with death. It's said that both remain at the home. Theophile Conrad is also reported to be one of the spirits remaining, being very protective and watching over the home. It wouldn't surprise me since Mr. Conrad died in the home after suffering a heart attack and falling down the basement stairs.

While most agree that Grace remains to keep an eye on things to assure they run smoothly, what most people don't know is at age eight she had a bout of rheumatic fever. The illness damaged her inner ear so severely that by the time she was twenty she had gone completely deaf. An excellent lip reader, few realized she was deaf until she was in her nineties and her eyesight started failing. She was a fiercely independent woman, intent on being in control of her home and her fortune. Having been born into an era ruled by men, this was a remarkable accomplishment.

Several months after Greg and I moved to Louisville we visited the lovely Conrad Caldwell mansion in old town Louisville. I'd heard rumors that several spirits inhabited the residence. As my husband and I entered the stately mansion on a late Sunday afternoon in November 2009 I certainly didn't think I would be coming in direct contact with one of the spirits, but I did.

Entering the front foyer, and turning into the first room on the right, you'll find the portrait of William Caldwell's grandfather, Gordon Caldwell. The painting immediately grabs your attention. That day, looking at the man's stern expression—his features forever frozen in an unattractive scowl—I couldn't help but comment, "I wouldn't want to meet him in a dark alley." I laughed and added, "Or even in a brightly lit alley." My husband and the tour guide both laughed politely at my poor joke.

Two years later, Margaret Young, William Conrad's great-granddaughter, would remark to me that Gordon looked so serious because the portrait was painted from a daguerreotype, which takes a long time to expose, so he had to sit very still. She also wondered if he didn't have bad teeth due to the lack of dental care back in those days.

After a short time we left that room, entering the area at the bottom of the front stairwell. There hung the portrait of William Caldwell. Unlike his grandfather, William's features are soft, warm and quite pleasant to look at.

Margaret would later inform me that the portrait was commissioned by her mother and uncle for the Conrad Caldwell Museum and painted from their favorite photo of her grandfather. She feels that the likeness expresses a lot of love, portraying a doting grandfather, which is how she knows her mother and uncle saw him.

That day, as I stood looking at the attractive portrait I said, "Now this is more like it. I wouldn't mind meeting him. He was one handsome man." Turning toward the staircase, I stopped suddenly as an unseen but distinctive hand caressed the right side of my face in what I perceived to be a loving manner. Then both Greg and the tour guide saw a chunk of my hair lift up in the air for a couple of seconds as if unseen hands were holding it. My skeptical husband chose to believe my hair got caught on a cobweb, causing it to lift up, but as the tour guide pointed out, there were no cobwebs to be found anywhere in the immaculate house.

I would later learn that there have been numerous accounts from people who have encountered spirits they believe to be Grace Caldwell and her father, William, on the staircase that we were standing near the foot of when my face was caressed.

Describing my experience to the director at the time, she realized my love for history and graciously asked if I would like to help with the upcoming Holiday Open House. Delighted at the chance to spend more time in the beautiful historical mansion, I eagerly said yes. That's how it came about that I spent time in the dining room and butler's pantry of the Conrad Caldwell house the first Saturday in December of 2009.

As I arrived for my stint as temporary docent, it was a gray day, which added to the ambience. The mansion was decked out for the holidays with a fully decorated tree in almost every room. You could easily imagine yourself back in 1908. After a steady stream of visitors touring the house in the morning to mid afternoon, things finally quieted down. Around 5:00 o'clock in the evening, with only one hour left until the close of the open house, I took advantage of the absence of the living and went upstairs to the bedroom reported to have been Grace Caldwell's.

Turning my voice recorder on and placing it on the edge of the antique bed, I said, "Hello, is anyone here with me today?" Silence answered me. I closed my eyes and taking a deep cleansing breath, attempted to reach out to the dead with my mind. It was a technique I had recently read about but had yet to try at that point.

I imagined myself floating on a bed of air. In my mind I said, "Come talk with me. Although it may have been my imagination, I could swear that I felt the air around me swirl with movement as if someone walked closely by me. At that moment I caught a Class-A EVP on my voice recorder.

'You don't belong here." The voice was female and had a gentle, kind tone.

Unaware I was making contact, I asked, "Is Grace Caldwell with me? Grace, will you talk with me?"

A light hearted, dainty laugh, not my own, echoed on my voice recorder.

"Was this your bedroom, Grace?"

A female voice responded on the recorder in a clear tone, "My home."

Without warning I suddenly felt a chill next to the right side of my body, as if a presence was standing between the antique bed and myself. I wished I had thought to bring my IR temperature gun. At that moment my recorder caught one last message from the gentle female spirit. "You go now. Please leave."

Even though I hadn't heard her request until much later when I listened to the recording, I felt like my time in her room was up and after a quick peek in each of the upper rooms, made my way back down to the butler's pantry just in time for a new stream of people coming in for the tour. But something about the butler's pantry didn't feel right. Briefly I wondered if the presence from upstairs had followed me down to the small room. But it didn't feel like the same energy. I couldn't explain why, but this presence felt confused and frustrated.

There was an instrument in the pantry that the butler would use to alert the family that dinner was served. It looked similar to an antique xylophone. As people had toured my space during the course of the day I'd played the instrument for them, showing them the lovely lilting tunes that would have called the family to dinner. Taking a breather between groups I heard the xylophone strike a few notes. Impossible! It was on the other side of the room. Clearly the butler's pantry wasn't as unoccupied as it looked. I took the few steps to the buffet where the xylophone rested. The air felt chilly around it. I placed my voice recorder on top of the rich wood of the buffet.

"Is your name Grace?"

"I don't know," a distressed female voice, different from the one I'd captured upstairs, replied.

"Are you following me to make sure I treat your home with respect?"

"Where am I? Please help me. I want to go home."

Hearing another round of visitors coming through, I quickly ended the recording, saying, "EVP session end." But before my finger pressed the stop button, the woman made one final frantic plea, "Help me now!"

For the longest time I assumed the voice to be that of Grace, since I'd heard the rumor that she was one of the spirits occupying the home. But two years later, after talking with William Caldwell's great-granddaughter, Margaret Young, I realized the distressed woman in the pantry that day was most likely one of the patients during the nursing home days. Was Grace the other female presence that I'd encountered in the upstairs bedroom? I couldn't say for certain, but I believe she was. What I can say for certain is that despite or perhaps because of, the Conrad Caldwell Mansion is a beautiful home and full of people, both living and dead, that love it.

6

BENJAMIN HEAD HOUSE

Prominently located on Main Street in Middletown Kentucky, the Head House, built in 1812, was originally occupied by Revolutionary War Veteran, Captain Benjamin Head. Rumor states that at one point in the home's rich history it changed hands during a poker game.

Currently known locally as Head House Antiques and Uniques, the property is owned by Middletown Mayor, Byron Chapman and his lovely wife, Freda. The property is listed on The National Register Of Historic

Places.

Hand-cut limestone, nearly two-foot thick, make up the exterior walls of the stately home. The front door opens to a wide entrance hall stretching from the front to the rear of the house. For several years, housed on the first floor was one of several unique shops, which was then the largest shop on the Head House property, spanning four rooms and part of the main hallway. As I was to later discover, the spirits liked their wares as much as I did.

The majestic oak staircase leads up to a landing between the first and second floors with large windows providing not only an extensive view of the property, but also letting in a more than ample amount of natural light.

On the second floor the rooms are leased to a variety of shop owners. Crossing the wide hallway to the back of the second floor, you come to a smaller staircase ascending to the third floor, with more shops and a room used for storage.

To the back of the first floor entrance hall is another staircase, descending to the lower level of the building. During Captain Head's occupancy this was the winter kitchen. When I first moved to Kentucky this space was occupied by a quaint lunch-time café known for their chicken salad and tomato-basil bisque.

Outside to the east of the house stands a small brick building that was the original summer kitchen for the Head House. Other outdoor buildings have been home to several up-scale boutiques, a Spa and even a barbershop.

~ * ~

While her partner in business and sister in law doesn't believe in spirits, Sarah—co-owner of then, the largest boutiques—does. While their business grew, Sarah would often tell her sister in law she could feel a spirit in the Head House. It was little things like items being moved over night while the shop was closed, or disappearing altogether and showing up a week later. Sarah got the proof she was looking for one winter night when she stayed late creating a new display. After she locked up and walked outside to get in her car, she looked up at the stately old mansion. Her eyes were drawn to the attic rooms. There, in the center window, stood a luminous woman dressed in what appeared to be a long white dress, looking back at her. As Sarah continued to stare, the young woman raised a hand, as if to wave, and dissolved right before her eyes. Sarah wasn't scared. Her senses told her this woman welcomed her and was grateful for the love and care she was giving her home.

~ * ~

I'd been to the Head House several times for lunch and to shop in their lovely stores, but I'd never done an investigation of the house. That was about to change. It was a few days before Christmas on that cold December day in 2011 when I took my equipment into the Head House for an impromptu daytime investigation.

As I stood in the main hallway of the large house, I turned my voice recorder on and set it to record. My intention was to go upstairs to attempt communication with the spirits. But like a Magpie, I'm often distracted by bright colors or shiny things. Located in the rooms just off the front entrance, the Head House's main boutique has so much merchandise it spills out into the main hallway in tasteful displays. A vibrantly colored hat with shiny notions attached caught my attention. As I stood there admiring it I caught an EVP of a young woman saying pleasantly, "What a colorful hat, isn't it?"

Not realizing a spirit had just spoken on my voice recorder, I murmured to myself, "All I need is a bright pair of gloves to match."

"Look in the back," the helpful entity advised.

Reluctantly I pulled myself away from the numerous shiny trinkets in the shop. Climbing the steps, I rested for a moment at the second floor landing. Closing my eyes, I reached out with my mind trying to find a hint of paranormal activity. The second floor felt as empty as it looked. Making my way up the back staircase to the third floor, there was a difference in atmosphere. The air was thick and held what I can only describe as an electrical charge.

At the left side of the small hallway was a door that had what was obviously an antique latch. The aged door was open just the tiniest bit. I pulled the door open and peeked in. The room had a slanted ceiling, proving that the top floor we stood on was once the attic. A large amount of items were stored in the small room, making it difficult to squeeze in the room.

Shutting the door, I began by closing my eyes. A futile exercise since the room was dark anyway. "Is it okay that I'm in here?"

A female voice hissed menacingly into my voice recorder, "No! I'm talking to Sarah about this." This is an interesting catch since one of the co-owner's of the shop on the first floor is named Sarah.

"My name is Terri. Could you tell me your name?"

The female said, "Margaret Ann."

"Can you make a noise or do something to give me a sign of your presence?" Instantly on my voice recorder a loud scream emanated that I didn't hear until I played the recording back at home that night.

After I came out of the room I stood there with my voice recorder running, welcoming the spirits to communicate with me. I didn't feel that I was getting any responses to my questions, so shortly afterwards I decided to call it a day. I extended my voice recorder in the crack of the attic door. "I'm leaving now. This is your last chance."

A male voice said, "Get out now."

Immediately the now familiar female voice said, "No, they are my company."

"Come back," A voice barely audible on the voice recorder called after me as I walked down the steps.

Once outside and seated in my van, with my voice recorder still running I asked, "Is there a spirit in the Head House? I believe there is. Can someone tell me who it is?" A voice whispered close to the microphone, "Margaret's house." It wasn't until recently that I learned Captain Benjamin Head's second wife was named Margaret. Was she the genteel hostess I'd been speaking with that day, as well as the spirit Sarah had seen that winter's night? Although I can't say with one hundred percent accuracy, I believe she is.

Once outside, I began taking pictures. It's commonly known throughout the paranormal community that orbs are usually seen at dusk or nighttime. To capture one during the day is rare indeed. When I downloaded my pictures at home I was delighted, although not surprised, to see an orb following me around as I walked around the outside of the Head House, taking pictures.

The orb followed me around the property that day, showing up in several places. An unusual green color, the orb was easy to distinguish.

Several months later I returned to discover new shop owners had taken up residence on the second floor. The ladies were in the midst of painting their space. Both being believers in the paranormal, we had a long, fascinating conversation. I told them some of the evidence I'd captured around the Head House and offered to give them copies of it on a CD the next time I was in the area.

Three weeks passed before I stopped by with the CD. Entering their shop, the expressions on their faces told me they'd already had some experiences.

Both ladies reported seeing a woman in a long, white, flowing gown out of the corner of their eye. Their concern was that she didn't approve of the renovations they were doing to the shop. They'd come in to find evidence of things being moved around when they knew no one had been there.

"Talk to her," I suggested. "Let her know who you are and what you're doing and ask if it's okay. Assure her you'll do your very best to respect her home and treat it with the loving care it deserves. She's really very nice."

Thanking me, they vowed to talk with the spirit as I'd recommended.

The next time I dropped by to visit with the ladies I was delighted to find that they'd done as I suggested and their items were no longer being moved around. They were still seeing her out of the corner of their eye, but not as frequently now. It would seem Margaret was accepting her new tenants quite graciously.

7

NUNNLEA HOUSE

Situated on two acres on the East side of Louisville, you'll find the Nunnlea House, a one-story, brick antebellum mansion built in the early 1850s. Both the mansion and its outbuildings are listed on the National Register of Historic Places.

Originally the mansion and 100 acres were conveyed to Harriet Hise in 1854 by her father Peter Funk, eight years after her marriage to Alfred H. Hise, according to the deed as an advancement and in consideration of the love and affection her parents held for her. A portrait of Harriet's father hangs in a prominent position in the wide entrance hall.

While Albert Hise passed in 1863, it wasn't until 1867 that Harriet sold Nunnlea to Samuel Wharton. It would remain in the Wharton family until 1887 when the property was divided with the portion containing the

Nunnlea house sold to William Hunsinger. In 1928 Nunnlea would again change hands when Jacob Owens became the owner. He would retain the mansion until 1925 when George and Virginia Eady purchased it. This is when the mansion obtained its current title, named after Virginia's maiden name of Nunn.

The Eady's added a mother in law wing in the 1930's, which was later used for the caretaker of the house. However, caretakers wouldn't stay long, citing claims of paranormal occurrences as their reason for departure. The Beautification League, who took over the property in 1962, currently uses a portion of the mother in law wing as an office.

The smokehouse and slave quarters still stand. While the smokehouse currently holds rakes, hoes and other gardening implements, the slave quarters houses a local Police Department. At first the police resided in the mother in law wing of the mansion. It was there that they frequently experienced the disembodied voice of a woman, whom they believed to be Harriet Hise. This was further substantiated by the occasional visitor claming to see a woman clothed in a long dress reminiscent of the mid to late 1800's.

Regardless of the reported paranormal activity, The Nunnlea House is one of the more popular sites around Louisville to hold weddings, receptions and other special events. The lovely outdoor temple can normally be found with a bride and groom standing in it almost every weekend during the spring and summer. If there's a ghost, couples in love certainly don't seem to mind.

Haunted or not haunted? I was soon to find out on a warm Wednesday morning in June 2012 when I first visited the mansion. Kathleen Owen had graciously allowed me to spend the morning walking through the mansion alone, in search of any spectral inhabitants. Armed with the bare bones of my ghost hunting arsenal, I carried only my voice recorder, camera and short handled dowsing rods. After a brief tour and history of the grounds, Kathleen gave me free run of Nunnlea.

I started in a two-roomed space called the Brides Room. This is the area where brides dress before meeting their groom at the outdoor temple or on the front steps. Standing in the middle of the room I turned my voice recorder to the on position and asked the usual questions of, "Who are you," and "Do you need help." Apparently one bride did need help because a female voice responded into my recorder, "Can you get me a hairpin?"

The most active location for me was the basement. Far in the back portion of the three-roomed basement the air held a heaviness. The wooden doorways are original to the building and aged to the point that the wood is harder than cement. As I stood in the back room taking pictures I felt something touch my forehead, almost like a tickling as if a persons hand was lightly touching it or a cobweb. I looked for cobwebs but none were to be found. I felt above my head, no cobwebs. The cobweb sensation occurred several times while I was in the basement and even though I looked for nonexistent cobwebs, the feel of a hand stroking my hair was unmistakable.

I made my way back to the section of the basement that held items used by the Beautification League for their teas, such as vases and seasonal decorations. There I experienced a sensation of cold air by my left arm that intensified when I invited the spirit to give me a sign of their presence by touching me. I asked the spirit to speak into my voice recorder.

"Who are you?"

"George," a male replied.

At home, listening to the voice on my recorder I came to the realization that that this was probably the voice of George Eady. He and his wife Virginia were the not only the ones to give Nunnlea it's current name but were also the owners who lived in the home the longest. It made sense to me that he would still be there.

Two weeks later when I returned, I went down to the basement and stood at the closed door to the older section of the basement, gathering my courage up to enter. At this moment a female spoke into my recorder, "Careful. Someone is coming." Thirty seconds later, my friend Pat who had come with me that day, walked down the steps to join me. After chatting for a few minutes Pat went back upstairs. I placed my hand on the ancient doorknob with the intention of opening the door and doing an EVP session in that area of the basement. But something about the atmosphere down there gave me second thoughts and I turned to leave without opening the door. As I did a voice said spoke on my recorder, "Want to go in? We won't hurt you."

After returning from my jaunt in the basement I caught up with Kathleen. "The last time I was here I caught an EVP I don't quite understand," I said. "When we were in the bride's room and you were showing me the wedding gown you have on display, a woman spoke in my voice recorder asking, where is the Lehman gown?" I explained to her I wasn't one hundred percent certain the entity was calling the dress 'the Lehman' gown, but that's what the name sounded like to me.

Kathleen gasped and a wide smile spread across her face. "I never told you, in fact very few people know this, but some time ago I was in the attic and found an intricately detailed, hand sewn, white dress, which I'm almost certain was a wedding gown."

I followed her to one of the reception rooms where, pulling out a small step stool and standing on it, she reached up into the high cubby, retrieving a large white dress box. Carefully opening the box and spreading aside the light blue sheet protecting the garment, she lifted the thin, white dress out.

Now it was my turn to gasp. "What a magnificent dress. I can't imagine anyone sewing all of those tiny button holes by hand."

"Look at that lace," my friend Pat marveled.

It was apparent someone—possibly several someone's—had devoted a great deal of time, energy and love into making this dress. I could tell by the look and feel of the material, that the dress was very old. Kathleen said she believed the dress to be one hundred or more years old.

Could this be the 'Lehman' dress the spirit asked about during my prior visit? While we can't be certain, my gut says yes.

~ * ~

It was also on my second visit that I met one of the policemen currently occupying the old slave quarters. He invited Pat and myself into his office and told us about the severity of the haunting in the mother in law wing. Often the policeman on the night shift would hear a female voice close to his ear. She would usually say one word such as, "Hello," or "Hey." On occasion she would ask, "Why are you here?" The police department had a difficult time keeping officers for the night shift, understandably.

By 2006 they'd had enough and moved the entire department to the building behind the house that was originally the slave quarters. The officer told us how he came into his new office that first night in the slave quarters and sat behind his desk. First he heard a female voice, close to his ear, clearly say, "Hey." Startled he pretended he didn't hear the voice. A minute later the closet door started to rattle lightly. As he tried to ignore it, the door began to rattle and shake violently as it the spirit was using all the force it could muster to shake the door. He couldn't take anymore. Standing and facing the rattling door, he yelled at the top of his lungs, "Enough! Get out and don't come back." As quickly as it had started, the activity stopped. He's never heard the female voice in the slave quarters again nor had the closet door rattle.

The Nunnlea house is a different matter, however. Even though the department is no longer operating out of the actual house, they still observe the ghostly activity. The policeman told us that almost any night of the week, around 3:00 o'clock in the morning, the house takes on a life of its own with the sound of doors slamming and lights coming on even though no one is in the house. He issued an invitation to us to come by any night to watch the 3:00 o'clock follies. We have yet to take him up on his offer, but the temptation is there.

After speaking with the policeman, I went back in the Nunnlea house to do one last EVP session. I stood in the main hallway, in front of Peter Funk's portrait. After announcing to the spirits that I would soon be leaving, I asked, "Does anyone here need help before I go?"

A male voice said, in a clear voice, in my recorder, "Need no help."

At this point, the hallway suddenly had an unnatural coolness. Even though my friend Pat was in the back office in the mother-in-law wing with Kathleen, I was certain I wasn't standing there alone. On a whim, I snapped a picture of Peter Funk's portrait.

Later I reviewed the picture and wasn't surprised to see an anomaly several inches below the portrait, by the top of the buffet.

Soon after, we said goodbye to Kathleen, and Pat and I walked toward the front door. As I turned the knob the female voice I'd come to associate with Harriet, said in a pleasant, genteel tone, close to my recorder's microphone, "You will come again, please." It sounded similar to what you would have expected someone of the 1800's or early 1900's to say when you left their home.

Seated in Pat's car, we buckled our seat belts as I recited my customary protection prayer, letting the spirits know they aren't permitted to follow me home. Then I thanked them for allowing us in their home and speaking with me. Before I pressed the stop button on my recorder I caught one last EVP from the male voice I'd caught in the main hall in front of Peter Funk's picture. He said, "Can you maybe come back again, little girl?" It would seem Harriet learned her impeccable manners from her father.

After such warm welcome by the spirits, of course I came back. In August 2013 I returned for an evening investigation with my research assistants, Diane and Ellen. We arrived at dusk. We went downstairs first, wanting to investigate the confines of the basement before it became too dark. As we walked down the small stairway, all three of us felt a cobweb sensation, similar to walking through massive amounts of thick, sticky cobwebs. A visual inspection proved that there wasn't a single cobweb to be found. Immediately I knew we were passing through spirit energy and that's what was giving us the feeling of cobwebs sticking to us. I explained this to my friends as we walked into the far room of the basement. As we passed through the original wood framed doorway, we all felt crackling static electricity and the hair on arms and the back of our necks stood on end.

Being the first to walk through the doorway, I was in the middle of the room when I asked the spirits to give us a sign of their presence. Being the last to enter the room, as Ellen walked thru the antique door frame we all heard a loud disembodied man's voice say, "Ask me."

Later, upstairs, I addressed the male spirit we'd encountered in the basement and asked if they make him stay downstairs. Diane, Ellen and I heard the same disembodied male voice say, again in a loud tone, "No!" I was fortunate to catch both instances of the disembodied voice on my recorder.

But as the man said, "No," Ellen suddenly felt someone standing next to her. She marveled that her entire left side felt like ice. We could see she had goosebumps and raised hair on that one arm. I took several pictures of Ellen and in each one there was an orb next to her. Our digital temperature device showed the air to be 20 degrees colder on the immediate left side of Ellen. We were able to trace the chilled air with the temperature device and were amazed to see it trace the shape of a person.

"Who is standing next to Ellen?" I asked. I caught an EVP of the now familiar man saying, "That's Harry." Upon review we were all convinced that "Harry" was a nickname, or term of endearment for Harriet Hise. That left us with one obvious conclusion. Harriet Hise had been standing next to Ellen.

Thrilled with the experience, we went into the main foyer. As we entered, I took my usual amount of pictures. I looked on the LCD screen of my camera and instantly knew I had caught something significant. I waited until the next day, after further review, to tell Diane and Ellen. But there in the foyer I caught a picture of a woman—a full-bodied apparition—with her hair done up in 1800's fashion, looking through my equipment bag. We could make out each delicate finger around the bag. Was Harriet Hise wondering what we were doing in her house and what was in our bag?

Before leaving we did a combination dowsing rod/EVP session. The spirits cross the rods as a sign of yes and uncross them for no. If they have something other than a yes or no answer, they speak in my recorder.

Diane asked if there is was spirit with us in the room. The rods crossed as a sign of yes. In the picture I took at that moment, a blue lighting rod of energy streaked through the small room near the rods.

"Who are you?" I asked.

"Jacob," the male spirit replied.

Reviewing the history of the house, Jacob Owen owned the house from 1928 until 1935, at which time he conveyed the mansion to George and Virginia Eady. Had those seven years been so pleasurable that he returned to the house in death?

As we left we caught one final EVP of Jacob saying, "Come back." We would love to.

GERMAN REFORMED CEMETERY

As long as there have been cemeteries, it seems there have been stories of ghosts haunting them. You might wonder why a spirit would want to hang around a lonely—sometimes creepy—cemetery. It makes perfect sense to me that the dead would want to keep an eye on their earthly remains, for if nothing else then to make sure the body they'd inhabited while on this realm would be treated with the respect it deserved.

With that being said, this is the reason I feel you have more sightings at cemeteries that have become run-down and neglected. It's my personal belief that the spirits are trying to tell you, "Hey, this isn't cool. How about helping a pal out and pull some of these weeds away from my headstone."

The spirits have every right to be angry that their final resting place has become over run with weeds and littered with debris. Not to mention their gravestones, which have become unreadable, crumbled, broken and forgotten. The spirits want us to know that even though they're dead, they're people too and have the right to a well-maintained final resting place. None of us want to be forgotten.

In a neglected graveyard you'll often find the atmosphere to be quite different from one that is well maintained and cared for. The air will have a darker, heavier feeling, even in the bright midday sun. And when the sun goes down? Well, if you don't have your big kid panties on, you may want to leave before the last rays fall on the horizon.

German Reformed Cemetery is definitely one of those cemeteries that give you pause, even in daylight. At one time it was easily one of the more neglected cemeteries. Now it's apparent that care is being taken to preserve the cemetery and restore the damage that time and neglect ravaged against the stones.

One of the four oldest cemeteries in Kentucky, German Reformed Cemetery in Jeffersontown is the resting place for many of the town's founders. Originally located on the left side of the German Reformed Presbyterian Church, that building is now home to the famed Thoroughbred Chorus. The oldest grave in the cemetery has a death date of 1814.

To the right lies The Lutheran cemetery with their oldest grave being laid to rest in 1833. It too entombs several of Kentucky's notable pioneers.

Today there is little distinction between the two cemeteries, other than the left side of the property suffering from considerably more decay to the point that several of its crypts are in rubble, despite being restored by the Rotary Club from 1964 through 1967.

Passing by the cemetery many times, it wasn't until Spring of 2012 that I finally stopped by for a visit. Sitting in the parking lot of Thoroughbred Hall, I said a protection prayer and flicked the switch of my voice recorder to the on position. Immediately I caught a Class-A EVP.

"Adam, help Adam," the female voice spoke. Reviewing the EVP, I had no idea who Adam was. I couldn't recall ever having known someone by that name.

Walking among the decaying headstones, I took my time, examining each one closely to read their inscriptions. One thing I've always marveled about with older headstones is the inscriptions carved into them. I'm not sure at what point we stopped putting witty verse on headstones, but I'd love to have one on mine. If nothing more, than to give people a reason to stop and ponder on who I was and why such witty prose would mark my grave. As I paused to read one such headstone, I placed my voice recorder on top of it momentarily. A voice spoke into it, "Don't leave it on the rock."

Later, reviewing that EVP, I felt bad. The spirits had seen their graveyard suffer so much neglect and disregard, yet here I was adding to their irreverence by using their headstone as a table.

Stopping at the gravestone of a man named Isaac who lived from 1829 to 1821, I caught a Class-A EVP of a voice clearly saying, "Isaac." Could it have been Isaac, letting me know he was still there? I have to believe it was. But almost immediately after that I caught the same male voice stating, "It was not her fault."

Had a female accidentally caused his death? Maybe a female horse threw him off it's back, causing him to fall to the ground, dead with a broken neck. Various scenarios raced through my overactive imagination. It made me realize ghost hunting often creates more questions than it answers.

Although it was midmorning when I first visited this cemetery, it was one of the most active burial grounds I've ever walked in. I would catch various voices on my recorder as I walked among the crumbling headstones. "Annie," a female said. Several minutes later, "We were only married one year." Shortly thereafter, yet another voice, "Vic Charles."

But it was the frantic female voice I caught as I was packing up my gear that left me concerned. "Help. Help Adam. He will need it." I'd started the morning with a female imploring me to help Adam and here I was ending my visit with the same female asking me to help Adam. Who was this Adam and why did he need help?

At home, as I listened to the EVP's, I couldn't get Adam out of my mind. Could he be someone buried in the graveyard? It would seem to me that he would be beyond help at that point if that were the case. Nonetheless, I vowed to go back and walk among the headstones and see if I could find an Adam.

~ * ~

I didn't make my way back to the German Reformed Cemetery until a month later in June 2012. My mission that day was to find Adam. While I did complete my task and indeed found an Adam, I also seemed to have found more than I bargained for.

Friends and fellow ghost hunters, Carrie and Tony, met me in the parking lot of the cemetery that morning. It was a beautiful early summer day in Kentucky, perfect for wandering around a neglected graveyard.

It wasn't until I made my way to the far back of the graveyard that I found Adam. A Private in the York Co Militia during the Revolutionary War, he'd passed away in 1832. Another amazing discovery was that his mother, Barbara, holds the distinction of being the oldest grave in the cemetery. His father, Andrew, also served in the Militia in the Revolutionary War and is buried a few feet from Adam's grave, next to his wife. Was this the same Adam the female spirit had urged me to help? I had no way of knowing. But in case it was, I bent down on one knee, placing my hand on the top of Adam's headstone and prayed for him.

As I prayed, I paused to ask Adam if I was pronouncing his last name correctly. A male responded on my voice recorder, "Hoke."

Shortly afterward, I made my way back towards the parking lot, where Carrie and Tony were waiting, having concluded their own EVP sessions in the graveyard.

As I stopped to tie my shoe, my voice recorder caught an EVP of a nearby female spirit saying, "Goddamn, holler when they're gone."

A male spirit said in clear response, "Don't worry, they're weak."

I've heard it said that negative entities hover around cemeteries that have once been neglected and desecrated. Although the cemetery was now being cared for, could this have been proof of that fact? I have no way of knowing.

What I do know is cemeteries are filled with spirits. And just like in life, there are good spirits and there are bad spirits. Some welcome you in their domain, asking you for your help, or chatting with while others merely want to be left alone.

When I stop to think of all the changes that have occurred over the last one hundred years around this small graveyard located in the center of Jeffersontown, I can understand the spirits annoyance. When they were first interred it was most likely a beautiful spot, surrounded by trees and farmland. Now, on a bust road, they have to contend with not only noisy traffic, but people like me, trying to disturb their rest. When I think of it like that, I'd have to say they were more gracious than I would be under the circumstances.

MIDDLETOWN TOY MUSEUM

Standing yards from the main house, some people do not realize the Stable and Livery are part of the Head House property and at one time provided shelter for the farm animals there. Some locals remember it being operated by Louis Brown who provided custom farm services to people of Middletown. Louis had several teams of horses and traveled by horse and wagon to and plow and cultivate ground for small gardens in the area. With technology changing from farm animals to farm equipment, Louis traded his horses and wagons for tractors. Tragically, when the tractor on which Louis was riding was rear-ended on Floyds Fork Hill, he died.

After standing empty for many years the Livery was later renovated into shop space for rent by Head House Antiques and Uniques. On the bottom floor of the building are two unique Boutiques selling everything from dolls to jewelry to high quality knick knacks and everything in between. The fact that these two boutiques are my favorite shops in the entire state and their owners my two favorite people, is another story.

Several years ago Mayor Chapman's wife, Freda, converted the entirety of the upstairs space of the Livery Stable into a Toy Museum. The walls are lined with thousands of toys she traveled the world acquiring. Ranging from toys made in the 1800's to present day, the large collection is continually being added to. While there is no charge for admission, a donation box resides on the wall at the bottom of the stairs for those wishing to contribute. The hours of operation coincide with those of the two shops occupying the first floor.

It's my own personal belief and experience that spirits are not limited or confined to a certain space. For instance, if a house is reported to be haunted, what's to say the spirit can't go out in the driveway and plop down in the back seat of your car? Someone once told me that they believed a spirit could go anywhere they'd been in life. I'd have to concur with that theory but also to expand upon it and say that spirits can go anywhere they want to. Therefore it came as no surprise when the spirits started talking to me via my voice recorder while I was still in my van in the parking lot of the Stable and Livery of The Head House

On a blustery March morning, sitting in my van waiting for the toy museum to open, I began my EVP session by asking, "Is anyone here with me?"

A male replied, in a voice loud and clear, yet only picked up by my digital voice recorder, "I'm Gus Henderson."

At first I merely thought, "That's pretty cool." But later, after researching Middletown's history my "Pretty cool" changed to "That's fantastic!" Because in my research I discovered that Middletown's first fire station was located a mere block from The Head House's Livery Stable. What really made me sit up and take notice was the person who started the fire station in 1948 and became Middletown's first fire chief; Gus Henderson. Mere coincidence? You be the judge.

Upon ascending the steps to the Toy Museum your senses are immediately on alert. I can't put my finger on any one thing, but it's apparent that you're not the only occupant wandering among the toys.

I'm one of those people who have a habit of talking to themselves, so finding myself alone in the Toy Museum, I immediately started talking to myself in addition to the spirits. I was duly impressed with the large collection of Tonka Trucks taking up not one, but two walls, on shelves from the ceiling to the floor. I looked at the trucks and smiled to myself, murmuring, "That's a ton of trucks."

A young girls voice responded in a Class-A EVP, "Tonka Truck."

Not realizing what I had just caught on my voice recorder, I continued to make my way around the museum. I was thrilled to see the largest collection of Barbie dolls I'd seen since The Barbie Museum. I'd never seen the Wizard of Oz Barbie's until then. My eyes rested on the first doll as I said aloud, "The Cowardly Lion." My eyes panned past the Scarecrow and the Tin Man, naming each one aloud. Looking at the fourth doll, I opened my mouth to say the name of the character when my brain took a momentary vacation. Shaking my head a couple of times as I tried to remember the name of the female lead of Wizard of Oz, I gave up and continued my tour. It's interesting to note that I had both my digital voice recorder going as well as my handheld camcorder. In reviewing the evidence, at that moment on both devices I caught another Class-A EVP from the same young female, this time saying, "Dorothy."

This was enough for me to believe I needed to call friends Carrie and Tony to assist me in doing a full-scale investigation of the Toy Museum.

~ * ~

It was several weeks later that Carrie, Tony and I were able to arrange our schedules to meet at the Toy Museum for an evening investigation. I was the first to arrive, so I went upstairs and explained to the spirits what we would be doing there that evening and asked for their cooperation. Earlier that day I'd had dental work done and my mouth was still so numb that I felt like I was talking with a lisp. I apologized to the spirits for my speech and explained to them about my temporary lisp.

At that moment my voice recorder caught an EVP of a female saying in a confident tone, "You don't really have a lisp Terri. I know, I had one."

Tony was the next to arrive. Carrie had called and was running late, so she asked us to begin the investigation without her. We started by turning out all the lights and sitting on the floor. I've found that when a space is darkened, often spirits are more willing to talk to you, not only via your voice recorder or camcorder, but also with what we call disembodied voices, meaning you actually hear their voices as they're speaking, without the aid of a recorder or other device.

As we invited the spirits to communicate with us we both introduced ourselves. With that out of the way, Tony said, "Now that you know our names, could you tell us your names so we know who we're speaking with?"

A male voice responded on both our recorders, "Pat."

Not realizing we'd just caught one of many Class-A EVPs we continue to sit quietly. Suddenly a disembodied voice saying, "Roy" broke the silence. The name was followed by two audible thumps in the darkness that sounded to me like footsteps on the wooden floor of the toy museum, walking towards us.

"We just heard a couple of thumps," Tony said. "Was that you?" His question went unanswered. Then he asked, "Is there anything you need?"

A couple of seconds later we both clearly heard a disembodied male voice say, "No."

After sitting in silence for a period of time Tony and I began chatting with each other. I told him about a recent trip my husband and I had made to Stone River, a Civil War battlefield in Murfreesboro Tennessee. Unbeknownst to us at the time, a male spirit with as much of a lack of geography as myself asked, "Is that in Indiana?"

In response Tony told me about his trip to Shiloh, another Civil War battlefield in Tennessee. I mistakenly thought Shiloh was near Washington D.C. and said as much to Tony. Before he could respond we caught an EVP of the same male spirit stating, "No, its near Tennessee."

This wasn't the only time during that investigation that the spirits would eavesdrop on our conversations and interject their comments.

Getting up, we both walked over to an area by the toy trains. Tony hugged himself, rubbing his arms. "I'm getting chills."

On my voice recorder a male voice advised him, in a cocky tone, "Turn on the heat then."

When Carrie arrived we turned the lights back on. While Tony stepped outside for a few minutes to make a personal call, I gave Carrie a brief tour of the museum. This was the first time she'd been to the Toy Museum and she was excited to see it. Carrie teaches the Ghost Hunting 101 class at the University of Louisville, which is how I'd originally met her. One of the things she does during the fifth week is to take the class on an investigation so they can get hands on experience with the equipment and employ the methods they'd learned in class. She and I stood in the middle of the museum discussing where she was taking her current class to investigate. She was having second thoughts about the location she'd tentatively picked and asked my opinion. During a brief pause in our conversation as I thought about the proposed location I caught an EVP of a male asking, "Would people love it?"

Walking over to the stuffed animal section Carrie and I looked at the large collection and commented on which ones we'd had as children. On my voice recorder you clearly hear a voice joining our conversation saying pleasantly, "I had the pink panda."

I asked the spirits, "Were any of these toys yours?"

The same voice that told me she'd had a panda whispered, "Not many."

Proof that our personalities continue even after death was caught when I looked up and saw a really cool object hanging from the rafters. I gasped and exclaimed with excitement, "Oh wow, it's a coca-cola bike!"

A male voice responded with obvious annoyance at my exuberance, "For Pete's sake, it's only a bike."

It's not unusual for antiques to have a spirit attached to them. Many people believe that if you love something dearly you can leave your psychic imprint on it. Other people, such as myself, believe that a person can be so enamored with an object that their spirit is physically attached to it when they die. The object could be anything from a house to a car to a toy.

After visiting the Toy Museum numerous times I firmly believe several of the toys to have attachments to them and have gone as far as to be able to narrow it down to the actual items. One of these toys is a large antique dollhouse that sits on the floor in front of the Tonka trucks. On the front of the dollhouse is a small ceramic heart with the name Holly written on it. I believe that to be the name of the young girl attached to the toy.

Tony and I bent down to look at the dollhouse. I was delighted to see the small rooms crammed with tiny furnishings. I saw a small replica of a stuffed moose head in a corner of one of the rooms. I couldn't help myself; I picked it up and mounted it on the wall of the living room where a plastic picture had previously hung.

"Get off it, get away! It's mine!" a young girls voice pleaded frantically on my voice recorder.

Maybe it was my sixth sense kicking in, because even though I had no idea of the Class-A EVP I'd just captured, I immediately backed off, saying to Tony, "I feel disrespectful coming in here touching this dollhouse. I can tell someone loved it very much."

"Yeah, me too. Maybe we should leave it alone."

As we both stood, taking one last look at the dollhouse I caught one last EVP from the young girl. Her voice taunted in a triumphant sing-song tone, "You can't play with it cause your not girls." Every time I listen to the EVP I can picture her standing with one hand on her hip, the other pointing a finger at us as she heckles us.

Leaving that area of the room, Tony and I rejoined with Carrie and made our way to the creepy corner. That's a name all three of us tagged the area that holds a worn stuffed monkey and two antique dolls. There's a distinct heaviness in that corner of the room that one would never associate with toys.

I can't say what possessed me to first put my recorder on the stuffed monkey's lap. But what a shock I had when I reviewed what my recorder caught after I did. An angry voice demanded, "You have that device on my hip. Get it off. Get out!"

At the time I said to Tony and Carrie, "I get a creepy vibe coming from this monkey." I laughed, "Maybe he's an evil monkey."

Tony said to the fur covered inanimate object, "So what do you have to say for yourself, Mr. Monkey? Are you evil?" Then poking the monkey's shoe with his forefinger he continued, "It says blue ribbon on the bottom of your shoe. That doesn't sound very evil to me."

The spirit hissed loudly via EVP, "Cut it out or I'll cut her."

"You know Tony, that monkey's eyes follow you," I noted.

The voice coming from the monkey had another evil warning for us. "I might hurt her. Keep her out. Get out, get out!"

Still in the creepy corner, I tore my attention away from the evil monkey to admire a well-worn antique teddy bear. I couldn't help myself; I stroked the almost bare fur in a loving manner. I don't think the bear thought too kindly of my gentle pat. For at that moment I caught an EVP that seemed to be coming directly from him. "Get out of my stuff. I hate you here. Get out of this house."

I caught another EVP of the voice coming from the stuffed monkey. He added, "And don't come back."

I made a trip to the toy museum several weeks later. I felt in my heart that I needed to make peace with the spirit attached to the stuffed monkey. It was easy for me to make fun of the monkey and taunt him, placing my recorder on his lap when I knew he didn't like being touched. What I was forgetting was that the voice talking to me was not that of a stuffed monkey, but a young man. And here I was taunting another human being, based solely on the fact that for all intents and purposes, their body was a stuffed toy now, while their earthly body lay in a cold dark grave somewhere. I needed to make amends.

I waited until the museum was empty and walked up to the monkey. This time I kept my voice recorder in my hand. My tone was somber and sincere as I apologized to the spirit attached to the stuffed monkey. I promised him I'd learned the error of my ways and would never again taunt him. I prayed for him and encouraged him to go into the light, assuring him there would be no retribution on the other side; only peace, love and forgiveness. I could feel the atmosphere around me change as I prayed for this spirit. And when I was done I felt at peace. I had done the right thing. Later, listening to my recording, I heard the boy speak. But this time the anger was gone from his voice as he urged me, "You come back again. I like you Terri."

In summary it's evident that there is paranormal activity upstairs in the toy museum. It's even possible that there is a portal in the museum, allowing numerous spirits to come and go at will. But whatever the cause of the paranormal activity, all the entity's there seem to be happy and content. And what better place to spend the afterlife than in a room full of toys.

10

MIDDLETOWN HISTORIC CEMETERY

Easily one of my favorite locations, this cemetery never disappoints. The earliest date of birth is 1731 and the earliest date of death 1812. There are many headstones that are defaced and unreadable, which are probably of an earlier date.

While it's obvious there is a significant nod to slavery here, I've not been able to dig up any facts other than the memorial placed there by the May Wetherby Foundation. It's inscription reads, 'In memory of Middletown slaves laid to rest here. 1811-1865.'

Although founded over two hundred years ago, the cemetery still accepts new residents. And in fact, it's in the newer section that I find most of the activity. Regardless of the paranormal activity, the Middletown Historic Cemetery has a certain air of peace. It's one of the few burial grounds that I have no problem walking in at night alone.

For the most part I've only encountered nice, pleasant spirits. But when I first started going to this cemetery I got on the bad side of a grumpy spirit. It would seem I was parking a tad bit too close to his final resting place. He told me in no uncertain terms to get out, both on my voice recorder and with a disembodied voice. When I stopped parking by the tool shed, which his grave was next to, he left me alone. When I had parked there he said things to me like, "Dirty hillbilly," and "Dumb bitch, get the hell out." So be careful about where you park in a cemetery, especially this one. I can tell you first hand, it's startling when you hear the words, "Dirty hillbilly," coming out of thin air.

Most of my explorations in this cemetery were daytime excursions. But one night, with nothing on television and no plans, I convinced my skeptic husband, to go with me to the cemetery. It's not that he doesn't believe really, at the time he said it was more that he hadn't seen irrefutable evidence yet. He's since changed his mind.

Daylight was rapidly fading and dusk setting in as we pulled into the cemetery on that warm September evening. Once Greg shut the engine off, his bravado seemed to dissipate and he claimed he needed to sit in the car to rest a sore back. That was fine with me, because I get my most compelling evidence when I'm alone. Slinging my camera strap over my shoulder, I pressed the record button on my digital voice recorder and made my way through the older part of the historic cemetery. Here were graves dating back to 1812 through the early 1900's.

I was feeling melancholy that night because I'd found out only the week before that I needed open heart surgery to replace a defective heart valve. Although I didn't admit it to Greg or my friends, I was very scared of not making it through the operation. But here, alone in the graveyard with the spirits, I knew I had an audience that would understand my fears about the upcoming surgery. I explained to the spirits that I needed open heart surgery.

"Are you having heart problems now?" a male voice spoke into my voice recorder.

Unaware of his question, I went on to say, "I'm so afraid that I'm not going to make it through this operation. Does it hurt to die?"

The same male voice said, "Can you try to have a little faith?"

When I later listened to that EVP, my fears fell by the wayside and I felt comforted. The thought of a man, buried six feet under, telling me to have a little faith; that put it all in proper perspective.

Meanwhile, as I later learned, Greg was seeing round blue lights flashing amid the gravestones in the area I was standing in. His first thought was that it was the blue light of a cop car. A few seconds later, when his brain was at full functioning power, he said aloud, "Oh, it's just the lights from Terri's camera. She must be taking pictures with a flash."

First of all I wasn't taking pictures at any time that evening on that side of the cemetery and secondly my camera doesn't have any type of blue light on it nor does it emit such a light.

Oddly enough, right around this time I was seeing a perfectly round, bright red-orange light in the aisle between two rows of graves on the newer side of the cemetery, hovering slightly above the headstones. "That's probably a round reflector," I murmured aloud as I went to investigate. As I got closer the light disappeared only to reappear in front of a gravestone a little farther down the path. I changed my direction and walked towards the lights new location. When I was perhaps four yards from it, the red light vanished in thin air, not to return.

I was puzzled at the time, but grateful I'd had the presence of mind to snap a few pictures of the light. I was pleased to see that I'd caught the brilliant red light in my pictures. That validated what I had seen in the graveyard that night. Were Greg and I seeing the same light, just in different colors? I may never know.

Researching possible explanations for both the blue lights Greg had seen and the red ones I'd witnessed, I learned that "ghost lights" are a common occurrence in graveyards. What ghost lights are is a topic up for debate however.

In the picture I'd taken of the reddish orange ghost light, there was also a large orb. I was shocked to see a face in the orb. Enlarging the picture I could clearly make out two hollowed out eyes on the orb and a nose and mouth. Researching faces on orbs I learned that many other people have caught the exact same sort occurrence in some of their orb pictures.

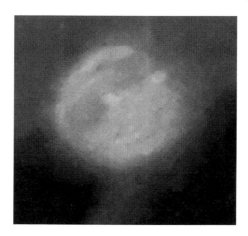

Later, as we were leaving, I could smell a strong odor of cigarette smoke in the car. It was an odd thing to smell since neither of us smoke. "Greg, do you smell cigarette smoke in here?" I asked.

"It's probably someone walking through the graveyard smoking."

My eyes panned around, although I already knew there was no one in the cemetery other that Greg and myself. So that shot that theory down.

I normally keep my digital voice recorder in recording mode until I am well off the property I've been investigating. This practice has provided me with Class-A EVP's many times. It would seem that spirits are as fond of a ride in the car as our dog, Moose, was.

I said to any spirit that may have been hitching a ride with us, "Is someone smoking?"

On my voice recorder a female voice responded, "He is smoking in the back seat."

Immediately after she spoke a male voice chimed in, saying, "Sorry." It was at that point the smell of cigarette smoke completely vanished.

~ * ~

A few weeks later I told my friend Carrie about my recent experiences at the Middletown Historic Cemetery. We decided to gather a small team and conduct a night-time investigation.

Although it was late September, it was a lovely warm evening when we all met at the cemetery three nights later. It was the perfect time to start an investigation as daylight was just starting to fade.

Carrie and I headed to the monument dedicated to the slaves that had been buried in unmarked graves from the early 1800's to 1862 as Chad and Jennifer veered off toward the older part of the cemetery.

"We're sorry our ancestors enslaved you," Carrie began. "You didn't deserve that. No one does."

A faraway sounding voice replied to her on both of our voice recorders. "Never forget."

Encouraging the spirit to make themselves known, I said, "Can you give us a sign of your presence?"

A female replied in a nonchalant tone on my recorder, "No not now."

We could hear Chad calling us over to where he and Jennifer stood, next to a neglected, almost destroyed crypt. It was so broken; I was expecting to see bones poking out of the broken stone.

"Stand right here," Chad requested, pointing to a spot near the foot of the crypt.

I shivered and I wrinkled my nose. The expression on Carrie's face told me she was experiencing the same thing. A stale, dank breeze seemed to be emanating from the broken crypt. The smell was that of something old and very much dead. The evening was warm, yet the air around the crypt was icy cold. The engraving on the tomb was worn and difficult, if not impossible, to read.

I extended my hand that held my voice recorder towards the ancient crypt. "Can you tell me what year you died?"

A tired sounding voice slowly intoned, "June 3rd, 1818."

Weeks later I returned to the tomb and studied the engraving carefully. While I was able to make out June 1818, I wasn't able to make out the day. I'd bet anything it was the 3rd.

But that night, comparing notes, it was at that point that all of us felt like we were intruding and had worn out our welcome at the crypt.

"Sorry, we didn't mean to disturb you," Carrie said.

As we walked away I caught a faint male voice on my voice recorder saying simply, "Go now, friend."

Leaving the crypt, we all decided to split up for a few minutes to go our separate ways and investigate alone. We find that spirits seem to be more comfortable interacting with a person alone, than with a group.

I walked deeper into the oldest section of the cemetery. As I looked down at the grave of a man who had served in the Revolutionary war, I heard a loud whisper in my ear as someone unseen, standing very close to me said, "Terri." Startled at first, I quickly regained my composure.

"Who are you?"

My question went unanswered.

Going on the premise that it may have been the Revolutionary war soldier buried beneath the ground where I was standing, I initiated a conversation with him.

"Thank you for your service to this country Soldier," I said.

I caught an EVP saying, "Your welcome."

"My son in law is a soldier. He enlisted seven years ago and has done two tours of duty in Iraq. During the last TOD he was in constant danger and we were all very worried about his safety."

"Is he okay?" The spirit asked.

Not knowing I'd just caught another Class-A EVP's, I continued.

"He's stationed in Alabama now. When he was stationed in Germany my daughter didn't come back to America for five years. I really missed her." I paused to take a much needed breath. "He's a Sergeant."

At this point on my voice recording you can hear the spirit say with interest, "Oh really?"

Suddenly I felt a hand on my shoulder. It wasn't scary, it felt more like a comforting gesture. I whipped my head around, but no one was there.

Later in the investigation I had my hair tugged and just as we were concluding the investigation, I felt a whoosh of air like a spirit was dive bombing me.

Weeks later, when I went back to decipher the inscription on the broken crypt I caught a Class-A EVP of a female saying what sounded like, "Help, Visit the Car's." The message confused me. Did she want me to play in traffic? I didn't get it. So I went back the next day and stood in the exact spot where I'd caught the EVP. I was pleased to find directly to my left, a headstone belonging to Henry L. Garr, born May 4, 1815. Sadly the date of death is unreadable due to the age and poor condition of the headstone. Was a helpful spirit trying to get aide for Henry? Who's to say?

11

LONG RUN CEMETERY

Long Run Cemetery, located off Route 60 on Old Stage Coach Road between Middletown and Simpsonville Kentucky, contains what is left of the old Long Run Baptist Church. That's not much unfortunately, just a crumbling stone foundation and a smattering of gravestones. But the ruins of the church are not what gives Long Run its historical significance.

The site's significance comes from its first titleholder, the grandfather of our countries sixteenth President, who also shared his name, Abraham Lincoln. He was awarded this land for his service in the Virginia Militia during the French and Indian War.

A memorial at the front of the property, dedicated to Captain Abraham Linkhorn (Their surname was later changed to Lincoln) states that Captain Linkhorn was working the fields when an Indian snuck up on him, murdering him in front of his wife and sons. One of the sons present that fateful day was eight years old Thomas. He would later go on to father our future president, Abraham Lincoln.

Traumatic events, such as murder, are believed to leave an imprint at the location. I subscribe to this theory and my visits to Long Run are the one of the main reasons that I do.

~ * ~

The first time I explored Long Run Cemetery was in the Fall of 2010. My husband was my sidekick that day, there more for the history than the spirits. He stayed at the front of the property, examining the memorial, while I ventured inside the fenced-in cemetery.

I set my voice recorder to the record position as I stood next to the gate. I didn't even have a chance to begin my usual spiel of "who are you, why are you here," before a spirit said in a pleasant, almost jovial tone, close to the microphone, "Ain't I a handsome sight?"

Unaware of the Class-A EVP I'd just caught, I went to stand next to Captain Lincoln's grave and asked in an authoritative tone, "Solider what is your rank?"

A male replied, "Captain."

By the dates on Captain Lincoln's headstone I could see he died before reaching an advanced age and commented, "People died young in the 1700's didn't they?" I heard a disembodied voice say what sounded like, "All the time." Later I was pleased to discover that I'd also caught the experience on my voice recorder and that the spirit really did say, "All the time."

Still by Captain Lincoln's gravestone, I asked, "Are you proud of your grandson Abraham?"

I caught a whispery, "Yes." I didn't think much of the change in voice at the time, but looking back on it, that was a completely different voice than the one who said, "All the time." Could both of the voices belonged to Captain Abraham Lincoln? In retrospect I truly doubt it.

I captured so many EVP's on my recorder that day that I became enamored with the area and returned more often than I should have. I bought fresh eggs every Monday from a local plant nursery, just down the road from the cemetery so I found myself stopping by for a chat with the spirits on egg day. It was a routine I followed for most of that winter and spring.

I soon learned that I could always get a response from the entity by the gate.; the entity I assumed to be Captain Lincoln. One day I asked him to appear in front of my camera. That day when I downloaded my pictures onto my laptop I noticed a misty shape, approximately the size of a human, directly in front of the gate, in the very spot that I was getting my best EVPs. And when I enlarged the picture, I could almost swear I was seeing human features in the area where a face would be.

Common sense should have told me that the angle of the sun caused the anomaly. But that didn't explain why after changing my position, the human shaped anomaly still appeared, in another spot, but still in the general vicinity of the gate.

Nonetheless, I still returned, time and time again. The lure of the possibility of speaking with history was too great for me.

I would frequently ask Captain Lincoln questions about the Revolutionary War. In one EVP I said, "You had to have been a brave man to be a Captain in the war."

He replied, "Yes, that's right." Then he laughed.

Although he was the loudest at Long Run, he certainly wasn't the only spirit there. Venturing to the back area of the cemetery one Spring day I found myself admiring the ornate designs on what was more of a monument than a headstone marking the grave of a young woman named Myrtle. "Someone must have loved you very much to give you such an elaborate gravestone," I said aloud.

"Loved me, yes," a female voice whispered into my voice recorder.

Another day I was admiring the headstone of a woman named Mattie, who lived a long life. "My Aunt's name was Mattie. I've always thought that to be such a pretty name."

"I hated it," A young woman in response.

I asked Mattie, "Do you have a message or maybe you need help?"

"I am happy," she replied.

Meanwhile I soon came to discover that if I stood directly by the gate to the cemetery I would get the best Class-A EVP's I'd ever heard, in addition to occasionally hearing a disembodied male voice. I foolishly assumed since this is where Abraham Lincoln supposedly died that it was his spirit I was conversing with. I felt honored that the grandfather of one of the countries favorite presidents was speaking with me from beyond the grave. The sheer thrill of hearing history straight from someone who lived in such tumultuous times boggled my mind.

Over time I formed a friendship with this male entity. That's when I began to get scared. Who was he really? He'd never given me a name even though I'd asked point blank many times. Was he Captain Abraham Lincoln? I was beginning to have my doubts.

I was hearing his disembodied voice more and more frequently during my visits and that had me worried. How could I be sure he was a harmless spirit and not a demon? I couldn't and that's what scared me the most. I knew I had to end the relationship and fast.

Something else was occurring which lead me to believe that the entity was not that of Captain Lincoln. I'm reluctant even to this day to talk about what the entity started saying to me as we grew closer. He started saying four-letter words of a sexual nature. He didn't say them in a cursing manner, he said these words in descriptive phrases of what he wanted to do to me. I found it hard to believe that a man from the mid 1700's would use language like that to a lady, even if he had been a soldier. And why was he always just outside the cemetery gate, never inside? Was it because he couldn't go on consecrated ground?

The final straw was the morning I bent over to pull a pebble out of my shoe and I felt a hand caress my bottom. There was no mistaking the feel of a large hand and the pressure of the fingers as they groped my backside.

Instead of being scared, I became angered about the situation. How dare this entity say these things to me and how dare he touch me in such a personal place and manner. In addition to the anger I also felt a violation. Strangely I felt disappointment too. I'd held lengthy conversations with this entity, I shared laughs with him and he'd claimed to be my friend. Yet this is how he treated me? That is not a friend.

I went to Long Run one last time, alone. I wanted to do an EVP session in real time so I would know what was being said at the time it was being spoken. To achieve that I would turn my voice recorder on, ask a question, wait ten or fifteen seconds and end the EVP session so I could listen to the results. That way I could respond almost immediately to any EVP's I caught. I was ready for hunting bear.

"You must give me your name," I began, "The power of Christ compels you. What is your name?"

"I am your friend."

"I'm not coming back unless you answer my questions right now. So one last time, what is your name?"

"My name is friend."

"Have you ever walked the Earth? Are you human?"

To this question I received no response. I point blank asked the million dollar question, "Are you a demon or an inhuman entity?"

After a long pause the voice said, "I like you, Terri."

That chilled me to the bone, so much in fact that I haven't been back to Long Run since.

So if you go to Long Run Cemetery, expect to catch your best EVP's right in the driveway by the entrance gate leading into the cemetery. But be warned about who or what you may be talking to.

12

BUFFALO TRACE

On Kentucky's famed Bourbon Trail there are eight remaining bourbon distilleries. In Frankfort one of these distilleries has been creating outstanding bourbon for more than two hundred years. Buffalo Trace has won numerous awards, including 'Distillery of the Year' seven times. Located on a picturesque plot of land where the buffalo migration once crossed the Kentucky river, carving a trace into the landscape, the property is rapidly becoming famous for spirits other than that which goes in the bourbon.

My paranormal experiences with Buffalo Trace began well before I ever set a foot on the property. When Linda called me to schedule my visit a ghostly voice came over the phone saying, "She's writing your name in the book. I will wait for you." This has happened to me perhaps four times over the last two years where when talking to someone on the phone at a reportedly haunted location a spirit will speak to me. I don't claim to understand the phenomena or to be able to explain it. All I know is it happens and when it does it usually means I'm in for a great night.

Arriving at Buffalo Trace, we started our evening at Stony Point Mansion with an arsenal of cameras, EMF meters, dowsing rods and digital voice recorders . The home was built in 1934 by Colonel Blanton who began his illustrious career at Buffalo Trace at the tender age of sixteen in the bottle room. By the time he was twenty-four he'd worked his way up to president of the distillery. It was through his leadership that the distillery was able to survive the hardships of the Depression, the Flood of 37 and World War II.

In 1959 Colonel Blanton died in the home he loved so much. After touring through the warm and inviting mansion you can understand why his spirit has chosen to remain.

Today the mansion houses offices for Buffalo Trace staff. It's not uncommon for the employees to report ghostly encounters. One of the most frequent occurrences is that of footsteps. A few people have had more direct encounters and have seen the figure of a man they would later identify as Colonel Blanton. My team and I didn't see an apparition at Stony Point that night, but we did see a chair move. As you enter the mansion, turning to the left you'll find the Colonel's study. Situated around the large fireplace are a luxuriously soft leather sofa and matching chairs. At the far end of the room is a large table with conference room chairs around it. The chairs all had wheels on them. As we sat on the butter-soft leather furniture with a fire blazing on the hearth, we would later comment that we'd become so relaxed, we forgot we were on a paranormal investigation. All we needed was a glass of the famous Buffalo Trace bourbon. Then I heard a squeaking sound that seemed very much out of place. Diane and I turned to look at the table and both of us saw one of the chairs roll several inches as the squeaking ensued again. The sound we heard was that of the chair wheels rolling against the wood floor. We watched the chairs but it didn't occur again for us that night.

While in the basement, as we walked to the back of the home to exit, I felt a hand on my shoulder. Thinking it was a team member, I turned to see who it was. There was no-one there. It wasn't until I felt the tell-tale tingling on the back of my head as the spirit energy again attempted to make communication with me, that I understood what was going on. I conducted an EVP session, but upon review the words spoken into the device were too garbled to understand. What I could gather from the experience was that an older female presence was the one trying to get my attention. It was unfortunate that we couldn't understand what she was trying to convey.

~ * ~

The next building we investigated was a dilapidated building known as the Riverside Home. Built in 1792 by Commodore Richard Taylor, this house is known as the oldest recorded structure in Franklin County. If you ask me, it should be known as the creepiest structure in Franklin County. Currently the two story building is too unsafe to fully enter. But at the front of the house and the back you can step into the home. I had no problems with the front foyer. It looked creepy, to be sure, but I didn't get any negative vibes, despite reports of the spirit of a young boy appearing on occasion as well as that of an older man. Although later, when reviewing my photographic evidence I could make out a mans face in the top of the doorway where a transom would have been.

It was a different story when I went around to the back of the building. I extended my arm into the room and asked, "Is there anyone here that would like to communicate with us?" Instantly I got the most horrific feeling. Shivers traveled down my backbone and I started shaking so violently, I thought I would vomit. Something or someone didn't want me in that space and they were letting me know it, evidenced further by the empathic, "No!" a male shouted in my voice recorder in response to my question.

I rapidly began taking pictures, knowing I wouldn't be able to stay at Riverside long, because of physical discomfort the spirit was causing me. In the first picture I caught an orb containing the ghostly face of a man.

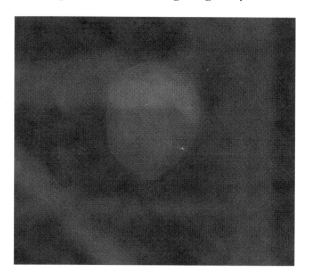

Was this Commodore Richard Taylor, the home's original owner? I couldn't say. But when I go back to Buffalo Trace I'll be visiting the Riverside Home again, but in the daytime.

13

MT EDEN CEMETERY

The drive to Mt. Eden Cemetery in Bullitt County, Kentucky is a pleasant one. The history of the cemetery is an interesting one as it originally was located next to Mt Eden Church on Mt Eden Road in 1820. After fire destroyed the church in 1879, a new one wouldn't be built until 1884. Mt. Eden was sold in 1956 when more ground was added to Fort Knox. At that time, Mt. Eden Cemetery and thirteen other family cemeteries in the community, which contained some three-hundred and forty-one bodies, were moved, and reburied in the beautiful new cemetery that the United Stated Government bought for the purpose on Highway 44, seven miles west of Shepherdsville, Kentucky.

The cemetery holds such notables as Isaac Skinner and his wife Elizabeth. Isaac Skinner was among the first settlers in Bullitt County, coming to Bullitt County in 1775. Also buried there is Evans Moore, who was in the last Indian fight on the Salt River in 1788, and his son William Moore, both salt makers. The cemetery is also home to many that met their demise more recently as we were to discover.

It all began in late September 2011 when my friend Carrie called me on a warm afternoon; excited about a cemetery a co-worker had told her about. Her coworker had explained the sad story of two young sisters that lived with their family across the street from the cemetery. On the night of January 21, 1983, their home caught fire, burning to the ground. Speculation is that the two sisters hid in fear behind the sofa. Sadly, both children perished in the fire. They were buried next to each other in Mt Eden Cemetery. Both headstones have pictures of the two girls etched on them.

Their graves are decorated with toys and various mementoes in an eerie show of lives lost at a far too young age.

At some point a house was built on the site where the two girls died. The current owners of the house report hearing the sound of young children running up and down the hall at night. In addition, they seem to play harmless pranks on the occupants as well, such as pulling all their clothes off the hangers at night and piling them on the floor. We weren't able to investigate the home, so we settled for the next best thing, the cemetery.

Carrie's coworker, Misty and her husband Jason met us at the cemetery at dusk. Carrie and I were discussing the paranormal claims, such as the girls removing clothes from the hangers, as we turned into the cemetery. Just before we exited the car I turned my digital voice recorder on. Immediately a young girls voice giggled on my recorder saying, "I took that hanger."

As we walked around the graveyard looking for the sisters graves I came across the grave of a young woman named Gracie. "Are you here with us?" I asked.

"Help me please," a female voice replied.

Finding the sisters graves. I commented to Carrie about how beautiful their grave is. At that moment a little girls voice spoke into my voice recorder. "Where is Eddie?"

Carrie set an EMF meter one of the girl's headstones. Tony asked the young girls if they would walk next to the device. I caught a very clear EVP of a little girls voice questioning, "Walk right past it?"

As we made our way to the back of the graveyard, in the old section, darkness had fallen and encompassed us, making it treacherous to walk at the back of the graveyard where there was no lighting. I slapped at my arm where a mosquito had latched on, not watching where I was going and tripped over a low gravestone. What's interesting is that just before I tripped, a voice said into my recorder, "Careful, there's a grave marker ahead." It's nice to know that even though we may not listen to what they say at times, spirits are looking out for our welfare.

Another interesting thing I discovered in the older section of the graveyard, was that the spirits there seemed to maintain their manner of speech even in death. As I stood next to the grave of a man named Robert, who had died in the late 1800's, he spoke into my recorder with a polite tone. "If you don't mind, help me, Miss." It made me wonder what sort of voices future generations will pick up when they wander the graveyards where spirits from my era inhabit.

It was around this time when I realized that whenever I took a picture of the area that Missy was in, there was a bright blue orb that seemed to following her. I felt like a kid with a shiny new toy and began to take numerous pictures of her. Always, there was this same blue orb. Clearly she had a spectral stalker.

After a bit, Missy and her husband came up to me. "Are you intentionally taking pictures of me?" she asked.

"Sorry, I didn't mean to intrude. It's just that you seem to have a bright blue orb following you around." I showed her the pictures on the LED screen of my digital camera. A wide smile spread across her face.

"My favorite Uncle is buried in this cemetery. I was born three days after Uncle Ronnie's birthday so everyone used to say I was his birthday present. We had a special bond." Her eyes shining with tears, she nodded towards the left side of the graveyard. "He's buried over there. He was in an accident and died when he was seventeen."

"Clearly he hasn't forgotten you because it looks like he's been following you around all night," I said.

I chatted for a few more minutes with Missy and her husband Jason. He was telling me how nice it was to get an evening away from the kids, even if it was only to walk around in a dark graveyard. After we laughed at Jason's remark a male voice whispered huskily into my recorder, "Where are the kids?" It would seem that Uncle Ronnie's affection for Missy encompassed her children as well.

Later, Tony and I went to the car to get bottles of water out of the small cooler I'd brought. As we stood there drinking the water I captured an EVP of a spirit saying, "Look behind you." Although I had no clue I'd just captured a Class-A EVP, I set my water down and picked up my camera, taking a picture of an area of graves behind where I'd been standing. I have to believe that on occasion spirits speak to us telepathically even though we may not consciously hear them because this sort of occurrence has happened to me far too often to be coincidence.

The next day, when I was reviewing my pictures, I could scarcely believe what I was seeing. Because after the spirit told me to look behind me, in the picture I took at that moment, standing at the back of the two sisters gravestones, was a little girl dressed all in white and next to her a bright white orb. Could this be the apparition of one of the sisters while the other appeared as a ball of energy otherwise known as an orb? While I guess we'll never really know for sure, my gut says yes.

Later, as we are drove away, I said into my voice recorder, "EVP session end." Just before I pressed the button the end the recording a spirit voice hurriedly said into the microphone, "Help me friends." Oddly enough, the manner of speech and the voice sounded exactly like that of the male voice I'd caught as I stood next to Robert's grave in the 1800's section of the property.

Once we arrived back at my townhouse, as we exited the vehicle and walked to my patio, I turned my voice recorder on and said a prayer of protection, in case anyone had followed us from the graveyard. After the prayer a familiar voice spoke on the recording, "Thank you for inviting me, taking me." This astounded me. I hadn't told anyone this, but before Carrie and Tony arrived that night to carpool with us to the cemetery, I stood in my living room and mentioned aloud where we were going and said, "If there are spirits here you are more than welcome to come along with us if you like." Sounds like one of them took me up on my invitation.

14

OCTAGON HALL

Located in Franklin, Octagon Hall has the distinction of being the only eight-sided home in Kentucky. The home of Andrew Jackson Caldwell and his wife, Elizabeth, construction began in 1847 and was completed in 1859. Andrew lived in the home with his family until his death in 1866.

A staunch Confederate sympathizer, Andrew was known to have harbored many Confederate soldiers at Octagon Hall, with quite a few of them being wounded. He would hide them in various places such as the cupola on top of the house (destroyed in 1911) and in a hidden passage beneath the front steps. One of many stories about the deaths in the Hall is the one regarding the wounded Confederate soldier who was shot in the leg and hidden in the attic. While he was up there, he removed his boot—which unbeknownst was putting pressure on his wound, thus staving off the flow of blood—and bled to death in the attic. It is also known that the Caldwell's used a portion of their home for a Confederate hospital during the Civil War years.

But the home's most infamous tragedy occurred well before the Civil War, in 1854, and involved the Caldwell's young daughter, Mary Elizabeth. Seven years old, she and her cousin were in the basement, playing in the winter kitchen. The children were poking at the fire when an ember popped up and ignited Mary Elizabeth's dress. She was badly burned and died a few days later on September 1, 1954 from infection caused by the severe burns. Her body is buried behind Octagon Hall next to her mother and infant brother.

In 1918 Andrew's widow—his second wife Harriet—sold Octagon Hall to an osteopath doctor from Nashville, Tennessee. Doctor Miles Williams would live there until his death in 1954. The doctor's heirs then rented the property to a variety of tenants until 2001 when the Octagon Hall Foundation was formed, dedicated to the restoration and preservation of this historic property.

~ * ~

The first time I heard about Octagon Hall was on television during a documentary detailing haunted locations. As I listened to the director, Billy Byrd, speak about the apparitions he's personally seen there I immediately put Octagon Hall on my bucket list. Little did I know that in two months I'd be experiencing the haunted property firsthand.

My husband and I have a tradition of going away for a mini weekend trip on or near our wedding anniversary. This was one of those times when he didn't tell me where we were going. I assumed our destination was Nashville as we drove from Louisville towards the lively town. But near Bowling Green, Greg veered off on a side road. Then, before I knew it, we were turning into Octagon Hall. I was delighted beyond belief. Being a skeptical naysayer, for him to have planned a paranormal weekend just for me, was huge and earned him major Brownie points.

Walking into the house, all of my senses were on alert. It was as if I was hearing, smelling and feeling spirit activity, all around me and all at the same time. Spying Billy Byrd in a room housing Civil War relics, we went up to him and introduced ourselves. We found him to be a pleasant and knowledgeable man. But what really astounded me was that he was a member of the zipper club, just like me. Upon seeing my open heart surgery scar jutting out from my cleavage he revealed to me his own open heart surgery story. I almost cried when he told me about some of his paranormal experiences immediately following the surgery. I'd had those same types of experiences. Sometimes it seems that God puts people in your path to help you on your journey and this was one of those unique moments.

I explained to Billy about my senses being assaulted by paranormal activity as soon as I'd walked in the door and after shaking his head knowingly he gave me the paranormal history of the house. I was delighted to learn about the strong ties to the Civil War. I was surprised to discover that to this day Civil War relics are still found on the property. In fact, just the weekend previous a man found four buttons from a Confederate Officers coat on the property. Billy proudly displayed the articles in the room on the main floor that he's turned into a museum, displaying all sorts of artifacts from the Civil War days.

Tears welled in my eyes as he told me about Mary Elizabeth's tragic demise and how he sees her occasionally, especially when he first enters the house in the morning. She will shyly wave at him and frequently say hello. Billy feels that he is a father figure for Mary Elizabeth and I would have to concur with that belief.

The stories of Mary Elizabeth are endless. Numerous people have given accounts with corresponding evidence of her singing, talking, moving things, etc. Although I wasn't fortunate enough to witness it, many say they've seen things moving around the fireplace where she was burned, in particular the arm holding the kettle, which is often seen swinging out on its own.

After Billy and my husband went outside to tour the outbuildings, I went upstairs to Mary Elizabeth's room. I was happy to see the numerous toys spread around the room, left for her to play with. What shocked me was the chill in the air. The room had to be at least twenty degrees colder than the rest of the house. This was unusual since it was a humid eighty-five degrees outside and the house was void of modern comforts such as air conditioning. There was no apparent reason I should be feeling a chill in the air. After mentally berating myself for not bringing my infrared temperature gun and rubbing my arms in a valiant effort to get warm, I began my EVP session.

"Mary Elizabeth, are you here with me?" I paused. "You certainly have a great number of toys. Which is your favorite?" At this moment, on my voice recorder I picked up a young female voice. "Stay out. They're mine."

Not knowing about the EVP I'd just caught, I continued with the session. "Would you like to talk with me, Mary Elizabeth?"

An adult female replied, via the voice recorder. "Wrap it up, a man is coming." This is amazing because sixty seconds later a man came up the stairs and poked his head in the room, immediately leaving when he saw it was occupied.

Continuing on my tour, I went into the guest bedroom. There on the wall was a large framed picture of Mary Elizabeth's mother, also named Elizabeth. My husband had joined me by that point and I exclaimed to him how incredibly beautiful the woman was. After he left the room I again tried to contact Mary Elizabeth. Aloud I explained, "We can communicate through my voice recorder. If you speak in it I can play it back and we can play games."

I caught the saddest Class-A EVP of a young girl saying in an anguished tone, "No! So how is it being that I'm not beautiful?" Playing the EVP back I was confused at first until I came to the realization that she might not think she's beautiful because of the ravages from fire that took her life. It's a strong possibility that her face would have suffered scarring as the rest of her body did. I made a vow right then that when I returned I would make a point of telling Mary Elizabeth how beautiful she is.

A short time later I heard an enormous racket nearby. As I entered the room I discovered a young boy, whose family was outside talking to Billy, had wandered away from them and gone in the house alone. He'd then proceeded to climb up the treacherous back staircase that has a large "keep out" sign on it. He knocked the gate down, thus causing the loud noise I'd heard. I picked the gate up and put it back while the boy ran down the regular staircase and outside to where the adults were. There was no one else in the house at this point. I said aloud, "Were you playing with that boy Mary Elizabeth?" The young spirit replied in a defensive tone, "He did it, not me." At home, listening to that EVP, I felt bad. In no way had I intended to infer that Mary Elizabeth was responsible for the young boy's behavior. I made another mental note that upon my return to Octagon Hall I would apologize to the sweet young girl and make amends.

Later when I made my way down to the basement, I discovered an opening in the wall that led to a hollowed out space under the front steps where Confederate soldiers were hidden during the war. I placed my voice recorder at the edge of the hole and stood there quietly for several minutes.

After thirty seconds something clicked against the recorder several times, such as someone tapping it with their fingernail to see if it was on. Then a male voice said, "Help me." Another minute of silence passes and then the same young man urgently says into the recorder, "I need help. Can you help me?"

This was one of many moments that I wished I'd played back the recording to hear his response so I could have prayed for him. So often spirits feel that they are trapped at a location, unable to see that they have the power to move on.

After I finished touring the basement I realized it was lunchtime and Billy needed to close the house so he could leave for lunch. I said thank you and goodbye to the spirits as I stood in the doorway. "I wish I could stay longer, " I lamented aloud. A voice spoke close to the microphone of my voice recorder, "Best you go now."

My paranormal experiences didn't end when I walked out of the house however. Walking around the property I kept getting the feeling that I was being watched. For some unknown reason I had the feeling it wasn't Mary Elizabeth, but a frightened and wary Confederate soldier. When I walked around the outside to the right side of the house the feeling was stronger. Looking up at the window of the second floor room portraying the Confederate hospital, I snapped a picture. Later when I downloaded the picture to my laptop, I could clearly see a face peering out between the curtains of the room Confederate Soldiers used as a hospital.

Thanking Billy for one of the most delightful days we'd had in a long time, we reluctantly left Octagon Hall. "I'll be back," I whispered as we drove off.

15

BOONE TAVERN

Listed on the National Register of Historic Places and one of the most unique hotels I've had the pleasure to stay at, Boone Tavern has the distinction of being the first hotel in Kentucky to become totally green. No, I'm not talking about green paint or green bedspreads. They recently completed an $11 million dollar renovation on the historic property that gave them the honor of becoming a LEED—Leadership in Energy and Environmental Design—Gold Certified Green Hotel.

To fully understand the beauty and historic significance of Boone Tavern, you have to understand Berea. Named as the Folk Arts and Crafts Capital of Kentucky, Berea is famous for it's Appalachian traditions such as arts, crafts, and music. The quaint streets are dotted with studios of local artists selling everything from sculpture to artesian breads to hand-woven cloth. In a town touted as the Dulcimer capital, it was no surprise to find a shop that crafts their own dulcimers.

The backdrop of the town is the majestic Berea College Campus. Many people are amazed to discover that tuition to the college is free. In addition to carrying full academic loads, Berea College students are required to work at least ten hours per week at Boone Tavern or one of the other 130 college departments and work areas across campus as a way of 'giving back' for the complimentary books, room, and board at the College, in addition to the education. But at no point are they required to pay any tuition.

At the Inn, all guest rooms feature handcrafted cherry, oak, and pine furniture made by Berea College students over the past one hundred years.

When reserving your room, make a reservation for the dining room at the same time because spots go quickly. The award-winning restaurant is famous for their spoon-bread and cornmeal pancakes. I can personally vouch for both. Another "don't miss" is their fried green tomato salad. Executive Chef Jeff Newman creates the most exquisite southern cuisine using local and Kentucky Proud ingredients. I won't torture you by describing the desserts. Just be assured, even though it's a two hour drive for me, I go back as often as I can. And yes, I have been known to order dessert first.

Boone Tavern was built at the suggestion of Nellie Frost, the wife of the Berea College president, William Frost. Previously, guests of the college stayed at the Frost's home. As the reputation of Berea College grew, so did the number of guests, until eventually they found that they'd received a total of three hundred guests in just one summer. Clearly there was a continuing need for a College guesthouse. Thus the idea of Boone Tavern Hotel was born. Named for Appalachian hero Daniel Boone, construction began in 1907 and was completed in a mere two years. Students were even to leave their mark in the building of the hotel and restaurant as the bricks used in the construction were manufactured by them in the College's brickyard, while molding, stair rails and other woodworking details were constructed in the College's Woodwork Department.

The weekend Greg and I stayed at Boone Tavern, upon arrival I explained to the desk clerk that I was there doing research on my book. She asked me if I'd like their Bellman, Fred Baker, to show me around the hotel and point out the paranormal hotspots. As he'd already left for the day we made a tentative appointment for 8:30 the next morning. I was told I was welcome to investigate any areas of the hotel I wished, as long as I didn't disturb the other guests. And she went further to invite me to come down to the front desk at any point in the evening and she and her co-workers would be more than happy to share their experiences with me.

After a truly memorable dinner in the dining room, I gathered my equipment and Greg and I prepared to make our way through the large hotel. We were staying in a Junior King Suite—room 203. I was pleased we had this room, since legend has it that the room down the hall, 206, is occupied by the spirit of a grumpy male that doesn't like people disturbing his sleep. Many investigators have made the assumption that he doesn't realize he is dead.

Greg and I conversed in our room while I inventoried the equipment I would be taking with me on my walk through the hotel. We were discussing the fact that although the room was luxurious, it only consisted of a bathroom and bedroom, leaving me to wonder if it truly was a Junior King Suite. "It would seem to me that the definition of a Suite would be more than a bedroom and bathroom," I pondered. "Do you think we got a regular room or a suite?"

A male spirit interjected into our conversation, setting the matter straight by saying directly in my voice recorder, "You got the king."

My equipment readied, I stood next to the bed. "I wonder if the hotel is booked up like this just on special occasions or all of the time?" I heard a disembodied female voice respond, "All the time."

"Did you say something?" I asked Greg, clearly knowing he hadn't since I had been looking at him when I'd heard the disembodied voice. Still, it doesn't hurt to ask.

He raised his eyes from the hotel brochure. "No. Wasn't that you?"

I was delighted when I played my recording back and discovered I'd caught the disembodied voice we'd both heard. Apparently room 206 wasn't the only room occupied by a spectral visitor.

Because of the obvious activity we were experiencing in our room, I turned the lights off and conducted a preliminary EVP session.

"Is anyone here with me?"

This time a male voice spoke into my voice recorder, "You looking for me?"

After our ten-minute EVP session we began making our way through the hotel, starting at room 206. Silence greeted my questions in the room. The air felt unoccupied. We made our way into the elevator to go up to the third floor. As the elevator ascended, a male voice spoke clearly into my voice recorder, saying, "Adam." Was this the spirit from room 206? Had he finally woken up and decided to join us on our paranormal tour of the hotel?

Another paranormal claim is of a young boy approximately nine or ten years of age who resides in the hotel. He is known to hang around the front desk, the basement and particularly near the ice machine in the kitchen. As Mister Fred would tell me the next morning, he also plays on the third floor. He told me about one night when a guest was unable to sleep because a young boy kept running up and down the halls in front of his room on the third floor. When the man would open the door the activity would stop. As soon as he would lay back in bed the boy would begin running again. Frustrated the man finally walked out into the hall, attempting to chase the lad and deliver him to his parents. He saw him peek around the corner and gave chase only to see the young boy dissolve into thin air. Needless to say, the man didn't get much sleep after that and left at daybreak.

Not knowing about this claim at the time, I felt drawn to room 312 for some unknown reason. I stood in front of the door, extending my voice recorder in the hall and asked, "Is there someone here with me? Could you tell me your name?" A young male responded, "Donny."

During the evening I took several pictures around the property. In the second floor parlor next to room 206, directly across from the elevator I'd gotten the EVP in, I captured the figure of a man reflected in the window. Clearly it was not my husband nor myself and there were no other guests there at the time, at least not those we could see. Was this the man from the elevator who said his name was Adam or perhaps the man from nearby room 206?

Completing our self-guided tour of the Tavern, Greg and I retired to our room. After he fell asleep I took my voice recorder in the bathroom and keeping the light off, shut the door. I could feel energy similar to the air just before a severe thunderstorm hits. I wasn't alone and I knew it.

"Do you need help?"

After giving the entity twenty seconds to respond, I pressed the playback feature.

"Help Rosa," a male spirit implored.

I tried to help by telling the spirit how they have the power to cross themselves over into the light. I tell them if they believe. The spirit interrupted me saying, "I believe Terri."

I continued, telling the spirit, "You are worthy of the light. Go into the light." This time he interrupted me saying, "Don't believe it." Clearly he was a conflicted spirit.

After the EVP session I got back in bed only to realize it was overly warm in the room. I got up and turned the heater off. I was dismayed to find it wouldn't stop running, even when I unplugged the unit. I called the desk clerk who immediately came up to show us how to turn the unit off. He was shocked to run into the same obstacle I had; even though the unit is unplugged it still ran. "That's impossible," he said several times. His only solution was to open the windows and have a repairman look at the heater in the morning. Thus, the unplugged heater ran all night. Oddly enough, when we came back from breakfast in the morning it was working fine even though no one had entered our room to do any work on it.

After an enormous, scrumptious breakfast of cornmeal pancakes and Kentucky-Proud sausage and bacon, I went back up to our room and gathered my camera and voice recorder for our tour of the hotel with Mister Fred.

He pointed to the spot in front of the front desk where he believes a vortex to be. As we stood in the spot both Greg and I felt a shift in energy. I'm not sure if that particular spot is an actual vortex but it's clear something is definitely going on there.

Mister Fred intertwined paranormal accounts in with the extensive history of the hotel as we toured the property. He told us not only about the hotels history but also that of Berea College. Then we went in the basement and everything changed. While he continued telling us interesting stories, the air had thickened and was considerably heavier. I could sense we weren't alone and said as much.

"Here by the offices some people say they catch the spirit of a young boy out of the corner of their eye," Mister Fred explained. "Maybe you're feeling his presence."

I didn't ponder it too much as we continued our tour of the basement. But as Mister Fred pointed out the laundry area I felt the back of my hair being gently tugged. I turned to scold my husband only to find that he was several feet away from me. At this moment I caught the sound of child's laughter on my voice recorder. It was pretty evident the young boy was the culprit of my hair being tugged and that he thought it a jolly trick to play on me. As we continued our tour of the large basement and made our way up the stairs to the Starlight room I could feel the presence following us.

Mister Fred nodded towards the ice machine in the corner. "We keep a scoop on top. The young boy here gets a big kick from playing around with that ice scoop. Many times the Chef or one of the servers will see that ice scoop move on its own. We're not sure why he likes that scoop so much but more than one person has seen it move."

I scratched my head. "Does it move noticeably like an inch or more?"

Mister Fred laughed. "It will fly through the air from the top of the ice machine to the other side of the room. I'd say that's considerably more than an inch."

Greg and I chuckled along with him, nodding in agreement.

Later that day, reluctantly leaving the beautiful, historic building with full stomachs and relaxed demeanors, I wondered, did Boone Tavern live up to the hype? Yeah, I'd have to say without a doubt it did. But just in case, maybe I should go back to make sure. And to eat more of their fabulous cornmeal pancakes.

16

HAYSWOOD HOSPITAL

Located in historic Maysville Kentucky at the north end of 4th Street, you'll find Hayswood Hospital. This infamous hospital has been abandoned since the early 1980's. Neighborhood residents claim to see strange lights in the windows and say they often hear the sound of crying infants coming from the desolate structure. Another of the many things people report seeing is a figure standing in window farthest to the left on the third floor. People say this entity appears both day and night. I was to later personally experience that claim.

Those brave enough to venture inside often say they see an old stretcher that moves on its own. Almost always they say that human shadows follow them throughout the hospital, while disembodied voices and screams of ghostly patients in apparent agony echo through the empty halls. Patients aren't the only apparitions visitors see, as many report seeing spectral doctors roaming the hallways.

Some of the less frequent sightings are glowing red eyes appearing in dark, abandoned hallways. It's rumored that the glowing red eyes belong to a hound of hell. This belief may be spawned by the strange markings on walls, floors and ceilings which are said to be warnings to visitors that they are entering a portal of Hell with no turning back.

This building and surrounding lawns has it all; cold spots, the sound of children playing, a strong feeling of being watched and an overall threatening hostility hanging heavy in the air.

~ * ~

My husband and I came upon Hayswood Hospital by chance, on our way to see what some call The Kentucky Slave House, otherwise known simply as Philips Folly. I knew nothing of the rumors of Hayswood at the time. We had driven by the abandoned hospital that afternoon on our trek from Phillips Folly to the Underground Railroad Museum. By the light of day the hospital looked like a spooky, yet interesting place to explore, so I made a mental note to come back before we left Maysville that night.

By the time we finished our tour of Underground Railroad spots with Jerry Gore, the owner and operator of Freedom Time and had a bite to eat it was 9:00 o'clock. Parking across the street from Hayswood Hospital, I have to admit, I was nervous. Truth be known, there are very few places that scare me. But something about this place made me nervous. I could feel evil intent in the air.

Greg and I got out of our vehicle and slowly walked across the street to the abandoned hospital. The second we stepped foot on the hospital grounds I could feel every hair on the back of my neck stand on end. I took a deep breath, mentally hiking up my big girl panties and began randomly snapping pictures.

There was a large wooden fence, approximately eight foot tall. I peeked through the crack between the two large sections of wooden gate and saw that this area opened up into a courtyard with a circular drive. It was obvious that this was the area where ambulances would drive, depositing their patients at the Emergency Room entrance. I turned away from the gate to see where Greg had gone, so he could come and take a peek. To my dismay he was back on the sidewalk.

I hollered, "Come and look with me."

He refused and implored me to come back to the car with him before we got arrested for trespassing.

I teasingly said, "Don't be a chicken."

He shook his head in obvious resignation and looked skyward, rolling his eyes and said, "Lord, have mercy on us," before walking over to where I stood. We didn't realize it at the time but a sinister male voice spoke deep and low in my voice recorder in response to Greg's comment, saying, "Punk, you're going to need it." And boy-howdy, was he ever right.

When Greg reached my side I turned back to the gated area and for the briefest moment, I saw a face peering back at me through the crack in the gates. Any other place, I would be running toward the gate, trying to make contact. But my gut was telling me to retreat. So, I did. There was no specific reason for me to believe darker, negative entities walked the grounds of Hayswood Hospital, but the gut doesn't lie, as I'd often learned in my ghost hunting experiences.

I walked to the left side of the building, immediately feeling compelled to take pictures of the windows; particularly those on the third floor. Unusual for me, I didn't want to look on my camera's LCD screen to see what, if anything, I'd captured. I had the strong feeling that something—someone—was watching us.

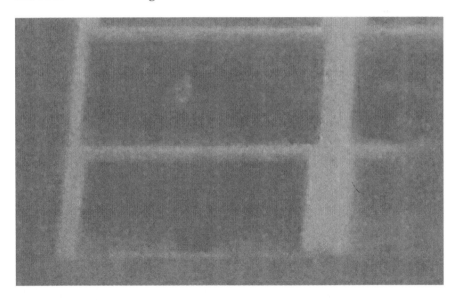

The next day, when I reviewed my pictures I was chilled to the bone when I saw a man's face looking back at me in the far left, third floor window. The very same window that countless others claim to see a man's face.

That night by the time I finished exploring the outside of the front of the building, I noticed that Greg had retreated to the safety of the car. It was late and we had a two-hour drive ahead of us so I decided to call it a night. I walked over to our vehicle and took a few final pictures of the hospital. As I normally do, I asked the spirits to appear in my pictures. But then I made my mistake. I mumbled, half under my breath, "Unless you're a wimp." The instant that phrase left my mouth I heard a far off, not-of-this-world, shriek and a big black shadow swooped down from the sky directly over my head so violently that it made my hair blow in the breeze it caused as it whooshed by. Instinctively I ducked as it swooped, then ran to the car and got in, slamming the door, begging Greg to leave immediately.

He got that knowing look on his face. "You got more than you bargained for, didn't you? When are you going to learn?"

"Okay, okay. Just get us out of here."

I didn't realize I still had my voice recorder going as we drove off. While Greg turned the car around to get us out of there I said my usual prayer of protection and told the spirits they were not allowed to follow us home or cause us harm. As I say that, I caught an EVP of the sinister male voice saying, "Too late."

The next morning, after we'd downed a pot of coffee between the two of us, Greg and I got in the car to go to the grocery. We were dismayed to learn the two-year-old battery in our SUV was dead as a doornail. It had been fine the day before in Maysville.

Our luck didn't improve as I discovered a puddle under my minivan on Monday. I was hoping it was nothing, but when I turned the air conditioning on and only hot air came out I knew I was in trouble. Taking it to the car repair shop that afternoon they told me my condenser was cracked and all of the freeon had leaked out. That was a bitter pill to swallow since I'd had a two hundred dollar air conditioning revamp job done only four days prior. I learned the hard way that air conditioning condensers, combined with labor, cost eight hundred dollars and change.

All week I had the worst luck. Anything that could go wrong, did go wrong. And to make matters worse, I was hearing strange knocks in my home and had an uneasy feeling I wasn't alone. After five long days of this I called a local priest and asked him to perform a blessing on me. After he blessed me the bad luck stopped immediately.

I am very careful about what I say when on a haunted location now.

17

FARMINGTON

Part of a military land grant given to Captain James Speed in 1780, Farmington was completed in 1816 by his son John, who with his wife Lucy, turned the property into a hemp plantation. Sitting on 18 acres off of Bardstown Road in Louisville, the architecture of the 14-room, Federal-style brick home was based on a design by Thomas Jefferson as evidenced by several Jeffersonian architectural features the home has. The architectural plans reside in the Coolidge Library in Massachusetts Historical Society.

John and Lucy's son, Joshua Fry Speed, was a close, life long friend of Abraham Lincoln. In fact, in 1841, while courting Mary Todd, Lincoln was a guest at Farmington for three weeks, recuperating from mental and physical exhaustion.

The design of the home is unique. Consisting of a single story above a raised basement, the main living quarters are on the first floor, with the kitchen and several servant and children's rooms housed on the basement level.

The front door opens into a central hall, which runs the length of the structure with a door at the back leading to a rear hall. These two halls give access to all rooms on the first floor, as well as stairs to the basement and attic. The stairs are hidden, which is a common feature of homes designed by Jefferson.

What I thought to be an unusual feature is that the first story is approximately five feet above ground level, with all of the basement windows completely above ground. Another interesting feature is that although the kitchen is in the basement, the dining room is upstairs. The kitchen is connected to the first floor dining room by a dumbwaiter.

Farmington has been painstakingly restored and is now one of Louisville's tourist attractions, depicting a 19th century plantation. Frequently used for weddings, receptions and various other events, Farmington is open to the public for tours in addition to being available for rentals.

While the docents at Farmington are knowledgeable and dedicated to sharing the historic facts of the property, it was our misfortune to get a "docent in training," one I might add that is no longer there. His facts of not only Farmington, but of the entire era was incorrect. He stumbled through his presentation in such a bumbling manner, that it became more than annoying—it became comical. Everyone on the tour laughed at the poor guy behind his back. The spirits of Farmington didn't seem to see it the same way we did, however and had little patience with him. In one of the bedrooms he pointed out the paint and said it was original. One of the people on our tour asked if that meant it was original to when the house was built or was a reproduction of a paint color they actually had in the room at sometime. He contradicted himself, stammered a bit and ultimately said he didn't have a clue. At this point a male spirit spoke into my recorder, "I've had it up to here with this man."

If that weren't bad enough, when we went in the basement kitchen the docent picked up a wooden tool that I knew to be a plane used to shave wood. Holding the instrument, he explained that this was a kitchen tool of some sort, most likely one to make butter with. At this point the spirits could no longer keep quiet. One spoke in my recorder, "I hate that guy!"

Still in the basement, I broke away from the rest of the group and stood in a corner of the large kitchen.

"I can feel you here. Could you give me a sign of your presence?"

Piled on the wooden worktable in the middle of the kitchen was a bowl of paper mache fruit and vegetables. Out of the corner of my eye I detected movement from that area and turned my full attention to the table just in time to see a paper lemon roll up the side of the bowl, over the rim and landing on the table before falling to the stone floor.

Did I see what I think I saw? I asked myself. Um…yeah, I did.

"What's your name? Were you a cook here?"

A female voice responded into my voice recorder, "Hermage." Then there was a brief pause before she implored, "Help me, Terri."

It always amazes me when spirits say my name. I've had spirits say my first name and I've had some say my full name. I've often wondered if they automatically know a person's name, or do they read your mind? Perhaps they read the car registration in my glove box? There have been many times when a spirit has said my name when I've gone to a haunted location alone. In that instance I know there is no way they could have heard my name from someone else calling it out, so how do they know? I chalk it up to yet another of life's great mysteries; or in this case, death's great mysteries.

What was amazing was at the exact moment I was overwhelmed with sadness as this spirit was talking to me, I could feel my arm being tenderly stroked in what felt to be an obvious gesture of comfort. For this woman to have suffered the atrocities of the horrors of slavery, to then attempt to comfort me—a white woman—proved to me the extraordinarily capacity for compassion the human soul has.

At the end of the afternoon I turned back to the large house. "You have a beautiful home."

"Thank you," a voice spoke on my recorder.

18

LOCUST GROVE

Locust Grove is a National Historic Landmark on 55 acres of the original 694 acre farm established by William and Lucy Clark Croghan in 1790. William Croghan was the brother-in-law and surveying partner of George Rogers Clark, founder of Louisville and Revolutionary War hero. George Rogers Clark spent the last nine years of his life at Locust Grove, from 1809 until his death in 1818.

Locust Grove also hosted three United States Presidents—Monroe, Jackson and Taylor—and was a stopping point for famed explorers Meriwether Lewis and William Clark upon their return from their expedition to the Pacific. In addition, Locust Grove was home to numerous enslaved African-Americans who lived and worked on the farm and contributed to its success. Today Locust Grove depicts the story of George Rogers Clark, early Kentucky history, and everyday life on the frontier.

Although owned by Louisville Metro Government, Locust Grove is operated and maintained by Historic Locust Grove, Inc.

~ * ~

Friends George and Allen toured Locust Grove with me in March of 2011. As soon as we entered the stately home with the guide, I could feel a female presence. That startled me, because I'd assumed if I felt anything that day it would be a male spirit, probably that of George Rogers Clark or William Croghan. We waited in the large front hall, while our host locked the door behind us, to ensure no-one would disturb us while we explored the building. It was then that I took my first picture and noticed a large white orb.

While some people scoff at orbs, believing them to be dust or moisture particles hovering in the air, I firmly believe them to be spirit energy in many cases. I've been able to ask orbs to appear on command, even to the point of requesting them to appear in a certain color. Dust doesn't appear on command. So the moment I looked in the LCD screen of my camera, I knew in the core of my being that the large orb was indeed spirit energy.

As I snapped picture after picture I couldn't help but notice the distinctive orb was following us around. Was this the female presence I was feeling?

At one point, when we were in the study on the first floor, I felt a breeze whoosh by my face so rapidly that it ruffled my hair. Immediately I took a picture, not at all surprised to see the same orb just to the right of where I was standing.

My senses were on alert as we walked up the narrow stairs and toured the second floor. But it wasn't until we reached the third floor that things started to change. Our guide was showing us the children's room, telling us what life was like at Locust Grove during that period. Without warning we heard the sound of heavy footsteps tromping up the stairs, starting from the first floor, slowly and loudly continuing all the way up to the third floor where we stood. To her credit, our guide never faltered in her speech as the sound of the footsteps became obvious to us all. But her face did pale significantly. She began talking louder in an obvious effort to drown out the sound of the stomping feet.

George looked at me, his eyebrows raised. I nodded my head, giving him a silent acknowledgement that I too was hearing the footsteps. I was standing in the doorway at the time and extended the arm that held my voice recorder behind my back into the hall.

Although we didn't hear anything further once the footstep seemed to reach the third floor where we stood, on the recording you hear footsteps walking along the hallway towards us and then a female voice speak close to the microphone, "Get out of my house. Get out now!" It wasn't until several months later when I was recounting the event to a friend that I realized that day we'd heard what appeared to be heavy shoes coming up uncarpeted wooden steps. That's fine, but all of the stairs at Locust Grove are carpeted and have thick padding underneath.

The guide appeared to be in a rush to get out of the house, once the sound of the footsteps stopped. So I point-blank asked her, "Is there spirit activity her at Locust Grove?" She seemed frozen for several seconds before finally answering in a firm tone, "No."

George, Allen and I shared a look, clearly none of us believing her. I believe she caught that the glance we shared between us because she went on to say, "People used to say a female spirit was here and didn't like anyone being in her home. But years ago we had a paranormal group come in and do a house cleansing and the spirit hasn't been back since." Um...no. We'd all heard the phantom footsteps. Who was she trying to kid; us or herself?.

19

ASHLAND

Known as "The Great Compromiser," Henry Clay was one of the most important political figures of his era. As a statesman for the Union, his skills of negotiation and compromise proved invaluable in helping to hold the country together for the first half of the 19th century.

In 1804, he began to acquire land in Lexington Kentucky for the purpose of building a farm for his young family. By 1809, Clay and his family were residing on the farm he so aptly named Ashland for the abundant growth of ash trees on the property. He and his wife would remain at Ashland until his death in 1852.

It's widely known that Henry Clay deeply loved Ashland. Many claim that his spirit still remains, wandering the lovely nature trails he had around the estate and enjoying the spacious rooms in his home.

Since 1950, Ashland has been open to the public as a historic house museum so we too can enjoy the peace and serenity Henry Clay so relished.

In the Spring of 2013 my husband and I spent several hours at Ashland. We were enthralled with the property and it's place in history.

Before we even entered the house our experiences with the spirits of Ashland would start. A specific spirit orb followed us around the property, both inside and out. Later it would follow us back to our hotel.

Touring the interior of Ashland, Greg and I entered the room depicted as Henry Clay's dressing room. I was looking at the picture of Mr. Clay's manservant. Below the picture was a drawing of an attractive young African American male. We were told this was the manservant's son. As the story was went, a famous artist came to do a portrait of Henry Clay and was so enamored with the beauty of the manservant's son, that he drew a portrait of the young man.

As I stood there appreciating the story and the drawing, suddenly I felt a male presence behind me, stroking the back of my hair. I turned to look at my husband, thinking it had been him touching my head, but he stood several yards away from me making it impossible for him to have done so. But I'd very distinctly felt a hand stroking the back of my head. I couldn't say why at the time, but I was certain it was the man in the drawing.

Another room with a presence was the museum room, directly across from the gift shop, where various artifacts from the family are preserved. I felt a female energy that was so persistent, I turned my voice recorder on.

She spoke urgently into my recorder, "Can you help me? I'm really dead. I need help right now." The woman sounded articulate, leading me to believe she wasn't household staff, but a family member.

Outside in the room set up as a smokehouse, I conducted an EVP session. The young male who'd stroked the back of my head followed us.

"I'm not deaf now," he said. It was apparent from the EVPs that he has no desire to move on. He was content to watch over the estate, which he loved so very much.

That night, back in our hotel room, I felt the young man's presence again. I took several pictures. In each picture the same orb appeared that I'd seen in and around Ashland. And in the last picture, although difficult to make out, was the shadowy figure of an African American male, standing in the corner behind the chair Greg was sitting in.

Does "The Great Compromiser" remain at Ashland? Possibly.
Do members of Henry Clay's household staff remain? Definitely.

20

WHEN SPIRITS FOLLOW YOU HOME

I can't say with one hundred percent certainty that I didn't move into a haunted townhouse when my husband and I moved to Louisville in the summer of 2009. But I can say that we never experienced anything remotely paranormal here until I started touring reportedly haunted locations. I'm only left with one possible conclusion; spirits can and do follow you home.

I can't pinpoint the first time I knew something or someone had followed me home, but it happened often enough that I started becoming more aware of my surroundings when coming home from an investigation. Eventually I started doing EVP sessions when I felt an entity had followed me home from an investigation. I was amazed at the responses I'd get.

It always began the same way. First I would hear strange knocks coming from the kitchen. Then, as I sat on the sofa, I would feel like someone was lightly stroking the back of my hair.

One time when I came home from a party in the wee hours of the morning I could sense that an entity was present. I grabbed my digital voice recorder and set it to the record position. I didn't get any response to my questions of, "Who are you" or "Why are you here." What I got was, "I like your outfit. You look good in pink." That raised my eyebrows because I was wearing a new pink sweater for the first time that night. I guess that answers the question of can spirits can see only in black and white or do they see in color. That night I started taking pictures in my living room, asking the spirit to show itself. In one of the pictures the mirrored background in my china cupboard showed a reflection of my couch. On the top corner—by the spot where I always sit—was a man's face. I was in the house alone, so I knew it wasn't my husband.

In one of the more recent EVP sessions I asked him, "Why are you here?"

"I love you."

Upon playback, I was astounded to hear that response. Although I didn't recognize the voice, it made me wonder if a deceased family member was hanging out with me. I pressed the record button on my voice recorder. "What is it that you want?"

He replied, "I want to be like you."

Add into the equation my ten-year-old granddaughter who asked me recently, "How can you tell if ghosts are around?" because she felt like she was being watched in our living room.

I can't say for certain that a spirit is still in my home, but when the back of my head tingles I no longer run to get my paranormal equipment, I just sit back and enjoy the feeling.

I've learned, when I get the feeling in my gut that a spirit is near, start taking pictures. By doing this I've captured so many apparitions. Often I capture them in reflective surfaces such as windows. It doesn't have to be dark for me to get photographic evidence of a spirit. Often I get my best evidence in the middle of the day. Such as the time when I took a picture of my office window. No one was in my house at the time. Yet I clearly saw a man's face peering between the curtains.

From the very beginning when we would swim in our condo communities pool, my young granddaughter would admonish me as she swam in the shallow end, "Stop pulling my leg Grandma."

"I'm not touching you," I'd always reply.

And I wasn't touching her. Often I'd be on the other side of the pool. But then, as July turned into August and I began to feel someone pulling on my leg when I was in the shallow end of the pool, I began to think that maybe, just maybe we had an unseen swimmer.

That first summer I tried to talk myself out of it. "Why would a ghost be in the swimming pool? That's the most ridiculous thing I've ever heard. A haunted pool? Hah! No way.

I didn't put two and two together until the next summer. I'd done my research by that point and discovered that yes, spirits can and do haunt areas that are covered by water. In fact, water is a great conduit and as some claim, helps the spirit to communicate. I'd go one further and say I believe water actually fuels paranormal activity.

I waited until an evening when no one was around. Taking my Gauss meter, IR Temperature gun, digital voice recorder and 35 mm camera into the pool house, I began my investigation there. Sitting in the dark, you are able to discern certain feelings more easily than in the light. For example, your hair being stroked, or a rush of air going past you in a room that has no openings for a breeze to enter. Certain things were unexplainable that night, like the twenty-five degree temperature drop on a warm summer night in Kentucky. I caught the usual array of orbs. And I caught an alarming amount of Class-A EVP's.

Sitting in the hallway directly outside the ladies room, I said aloud, "I smell stale cigarette smoke. I wonder if somebody's been smoking in the bathroom?"

"Must have been teenagers," an older woman's voice answered me.

Unaware of the EVP I'd just captured, I stood up, brushed off the back of my shorts and started to head out to the pool area.

"I'm right behind you," the same woman informed me in a matter of fact tone on my voice recorder.

Opening the door and walking out to the pool deck, I set my voice recorder on one of the patio tables surrounding the pool as I adjusted the settings on my camera.

"Where's Michael?" A young woman asked, her voice full of alarm, close to the microphone.

My camera adjusted, I picked my voice recorder up and held it towards the shallow end of the pool. "Did you die here?"

A female voice with a British accent replied, "Would you place your whole family under the water? I did."

"If you speak into this black device I'll be able to communicate with you," I said.

The same female said, "I already did."

Still standing next to the pool, I asked, "Who touched my granddaughter's leg in the pool last summer?" A male voice said via my recorder, "Who touched Jasmine?" A female answered, saying, "That was me." This EVP conversation was especially interesting to me because I'd not mentioned my granddaughter by name at all that night.

Unaware of the phenomenal exchange I was having with these entities via EVP, I continued the session and asked, "Are your bones buried here?" A female voice replied, "I died here."

Ending the session, I was in the hallway of the pool house leaving and I said, "Well I have to go, I have a pork roast in the oven. Goodbye, EVP session end." A pleasant female voice replied, "Goodbye," while a male voice interjected in a wistful tone, "I loved pork."

~ * ~

Several days later I felt eyes watching me as I gardened. Again, grabbing my camera and snapping pictures, I wasn't at all surprised to see a young boy. He was standing to the left of my electric meter near my patio, staring straight at me.

Over time it became increasingly clear to me that spirits are—for whatever reason—drawn to me. Am I a conduit? Am I a medium? Is the fact that Kentucky is built on a bed of limestone the reason I veil between life and death is thinner for me? To this day I have no clue. But whatever I am, it's become clear that I'm a beacon of light in a dark tunnel for the spirits. The spirit of an Indian woman once said to me, when I asked if she knew who I was, "Wolfshana." It was an Indian word I later learned means Spirit. Was she trying to tell me I'm a spirit walker with one foot on each side of the veil? With three near death experiences under my belt it's very possible. Or could my interactions with the spirits be the result of what a male spirit at Tom Sawyer Park recently told me? His words to me were simply, "You care."

21

ORBS

When discussing the paranormal, easily the most controversial subject—one both believers and nonbelievers have an opinion on—are orbs. Presumed to be manifestations of spirit energy, many claim orbs to be dust particles, rain droplets or flying insects. Although I'm a firm believer in orbs, I do think that in many instances what we presume to be orbs are indeed, not. But I also firmly believe there are cases where we do see and catch evidence of true orbs.

One of the things I do in an active location is ask the spirits to show themselves in front of my camera. Often, upon asking, bright orbs will appear. Combined with EVP evidence captured at the same time, I know I've caught a true orb.

Could spirits show up as a specific colored orb upon request? I'd never heard of such a thing, but I didn't see why they couldn't. I conducted a test in a well known haunted location. I asked a spirit to show up as a green orb. I pointed to the area I wanted them to manifest. I waited five seconds and took a picture. Upon reviewing the picture, sure enough, there was a bright green orb in the exact spot I'd requested. I've yet to see a spec of dust change to a specific color upon request.

To be able to ascertain a true orb, you need to learn to debunk them. One of the ways an orb can clearly be debunked is to enlarge the photo of the orb. Is the orb behind an object? Dust, flying insect or any other foreign particle couldn't have caused the orb anomaly because of the flash from the camera. If you see an orb behind an object go back and measure how far the orb would have been from you when you took the photo. Dust orbs are created when the dust particle is very close to the lens and in no way can dust produce an orb if it is more than 2 feet away from the lens.

Try to recreate dust orbs, so you can see what they look like and thus be able to negate them from pictures where you otherwise may have thought of them as a true orb. More often than not, dust orbs will be in multitudes.

Does the orb cast a shadow? In studying orbs, I've tried to recreate them by purposefully taking pictures of flying insects at night with a flash. In every case they've created a shadow. Also bugs tend to appear very bright, similar to what a bike reflector would like if you used your flash when photographing it. And they are normally an odd shape, not perfectly round as most spirit orbs.

Another question to always ask is if other evidence was captured on or at the same time of the supposed orb. Did you catch an EVP, or have a sudden blast of cold air surround the area for no apparent reason? When analyzing anomalies you capture on film, you need to take in account all available data of what was occurring at that moment in order to make an educated opinion.

When you see orb-like anomalies, it's almost always on pictures taken at night. So when you catch what appears to be an orb, during daylight, it's often the real deal and something to be excited about. Even being a self proclaimed ghost magnet, it's the rare occurrence when I capture such an orb. And when I do catch an orb during the day, I never automatically assume it to be a true orb. Take your time and follow the steps of trying to recreate the anomaly. And always—as I previously stated—take all available data into account.

One thing all investigators can agree on is ghost hunting is not an exact science. Much of what we experience is a feeling, or gut reaction. Learn to trust your instincts when ghost hunting. The gut never lies.

~ * ~

I'm often asked if the color of an orb has any significance. Does red mean it's the energy of an angry spirit? Does blue represent a spirit that is overcome with sadness? We may never know the truth to orbs until we are spirit energy ourselves, and by then, will it really matter to us?

Colors of Orbs

```
PINK -------------------- Openness
RED ----------------------- Stress
DARK RED ------------------ Anger
ORANGE ------------- Healing Energy
YELLOW ------------------ Caution
GREEN ------------------- Fertility
LIGHT BLUE ------------- Tranquility
DARK BLUE -------- Shielding, Shyness
LAVENDER --------- At peace with God
WHITE ---- Protection, High Frequency
```

I can only give you my own personal beliefs. I believe that the color of an orb is similar to an aura. They say every living thing produces an aura so why should spirit energy be any different?

To determine the why an orb may show up as a specific color, I first studied auras. What I learned amazed me. Our aura's are different colors depending on our mood and personality. The result of my research was that it's very possible and probable certain colors represent how a spirit is feeling at a specific point in time.

Orbs will always be a controversial subject. Dust? water droplets? Spirit Energy? You be the judge.

22

ELECTRONIC VOICE PHENOMENON

While some of my evidence is comprised of personal experiences, the bulk of it is auditory, closely followed by photographic.

Photographic evidence is the easiest to explain. You see an anomaly in your picture and you believe it to be that of a spirit. We matrix with our eyes as well as our ears, so it could be shadows formed in a particular pattern that makes us think we are seeing a spirit. Or it could just possibly be an actual spirit. Photographic evidence is among the most debated, whether it's apparitions or the highly controversial orb.

Auditory evidence has been labeled and cataloged in specific classifications under the main category of Electronic Voice Phenomenon. You may know this by its more common label of EVP.

EVP is a method in which you capture a spirit's voice by using a regular recording device such as the digital voice recorder. Spirit voices can also be recorded on camcorders. A common practice in the field is to cross-check EVP evidence to see if the sound was imprinted on all recording devices being employed at the time. A good example is my investigation of the Toy Museum where I caught the same spirit voice on both my digital voice recorder and camcorder. You might think it elementary that the same evidence would be caught on all devices, but oddly, a spirit voice isn't usually caught on all recording devices running at the same time. For instance, all four investigators can be standing together, all with voice recorders running and only one will capture an EVP, despite it being a clear Class-A EVP.

~ * ~

There are three classifications of EVP are A, B and C, explained as follows;

Class A – An EVP that everyone who listens to it can clearly hear and understand what is being said. This type of EVP doesn't need any type of enhancement or manipulation in order for everyone to heard it with ease.

Class B – This EVP is best heard and understood after enhancement with EVP software. It could be that the sound byte needs to be amplified, or more common that background noise needs to be eliminated.

Class C – The type most often caught by investigators, these are hard to understand without enhancement, and often even with it. This EVP is open to interpretation, as usually everyone seems to hear something different being said. Most investigators don't bother to waste their time with Class C EVP's.

Capturing an EVP is a simple, straightforward process. The most common device currently used to obtain EVP's is the popular digital voice recorder. The general rule of thumb is to press the record button and wait a couple of seconds before stating the date and location of the recording.

Don't speak loudly, if you value your eardrums. Today's recording devices capture even the faintest breath, so if you ask your questions in a loud tone, you'll likely have painful ears after reviewing the recordings. This is something all of us in the field experience more often than we should. By the same token, never whisper or speak softly. The reasoning behind this is because if you speak in a soft tone, your voice may be mistaken for that of a spirit. You'd be surprised at how many times this happens, even by seasoned professionals.

Ask the spirit a question and then *shut your mouth*. There is nothing more frustrating then to hear a spirit start to speak, but have the investigator immediately ask another question, drowning out the spirits voice. A good rule of thumb is to silently count to ten, in order to give the spirit a chance to reply. In life we often respond quickly to a question. But for whatever reason, spirits don't seem to be able to respond as rapidly. If you think about the sheer amount of energy and force it takes for a spirit to be able to cross the veil and interact in our realm, it's no wonder it takes several seconds for them to respond.

Be respectful of the spirits you're attempting to contact. You are in their space; their home. Whether dead or alive, imagine a stranger coming in your home, demanding you answer their questions. Keeping that rule in mind, be gracious and thank them for allowing you to be in their space. I try to always thank the spirits at the end of an EVP session for their time and cooperation. Common courtesy can go a long way in the paranormal field. Imagine yourself in their shoes. They are after all, people too, just in another form. While they no longer have the aid of a physical body, they are the same person they were when they inhabited a living body.

At the end of my recording session I always say, "EVP session end." Then I silently count to ten, to give the spirit an opportunity to say any last words before I press the button to stop the recording. I almost always capture an EVP after saying, "EVP session end." Sometimes it's as simple as, "Thank you," or, "Goodbye." Or at times it's a thought-provoking message such as, "I loved pork." The main thing I find is that spirits love having the last word.

Location of your recording device can add another level of success to your EVP evidence. For instance, when I'm in a cemetery I'll often place my recorder on top of a person's headstone while I ask questions. More often than not, I get clear responses. I've learned the hard way that if you see an above ground crypt that has a wide crack in it, never place your voice recorder in the opening. You'll be likely to get more than you bargained for.

In the case of the haunted toy museum I frequently placed my recorder on the laps of stuffed animals or the tops of dollhouses and even in the beds of toy pickup trucks. By doing this I was able to discover several toys that have spirit attachments. In that instance I guess you could say EVP's are like real estate. Location, location, location.

Your ultimate success in capturing a multitude of EVPs can be summarized in one word—intent. If you are trying to capture EVPs in order to have a good scare, or other entertainment, forget it. The only EVP you'll be likely to get is of a darker nature. But if you go into it with goodness in your heart and from the standpoint of wanting to help someone who may be stuck in a plane of existence they should have moved on from, then you are likely to have enormous success.

It's a common belief that spirits can hear your thoughts and I would have to concur. So don't think you can pull one over on them and make them think you have the best intentions when you don't. They'll find you out each and every time and react with a wrath that you may not like.

Spirits are merely disembodied people with the same soul that had when they were in their physical body. We are all made of energy and it's a scientific fact that energy never dies. So how arrogant it would be for us not to believe in life after physical death. So the next time you hunt for EVPs, keep in mind that they are people too and treat them as such. You wouldn't go into their home and demand they talk to you and answer your questions when they were alive, so why do you presume to do that once their body dies? Be respectful and treat spirits the same way you would want to be treated and see if you don't start getting phenomenal responses.

23

PARANORMAL TERMINOLOGY

Anomaly is an irregular, unusual or abnormal event that doesn't fit a standard rule or law; something unexplainable.

Apparition a spirit appearing to us in human form. Or in the case of an animal, the form they were in during life. This occurrence isn't limited to humans and animals. Apparitions of ships, trains, cars, and other inanimate objects have been seen.

Apport happens when a solid object appears, seemingly out of nowhere, with the assistance of a spirit.

Aura is what we call the energy field that surrounds all living things. Each Aura is unique to that person, animal or plant.

Automatic Writing is when a spirit takes control of the writer's hand and writes out a message. The belief is that you are channeling a spirit and writing their thoughts and words.

Channeling is when a person allows a spirit to use them temporarily to communicate information.

Cross-species Communication is when you have a special rapport with animals, plants or alien beings, to the point that you understand what they are thinking and feeling.

Crystallomancy is the art of gazing into a crystal globe, pool of water, mirror, or any transparent object, in order to see visions or to summon forth spirits. The person may sometimes put themselves into a hypnotic state to achieve this.

Clairaudience is the ability to hear the voices of spirits or other paranormal sounds inaudible to the human ear.

Clairvoyance is the ability to see specific events in the future or the past. To have clear visual mental images of auras and other psychic phenomena.

Conduit is a person, object or place that draws spirit energy to it. A person is believed to be a conduit after a NDE (Near Death Experience).

Dejà Vu is an event that feels as if you are re-experiencing it or as if it has happened at another time.

Divination is to obtain unknown knowledge or future events from omens. Astrology is often considered divination.

Demonologist is a person who specializes in the removal of evil or demonic forces from a given environment.

Demonology is the study of demons.

Doppelganger is the spirit of a living person outside of their physical body. Some call it a spirit twin or clone.

Dowsing is the practice of seeking answers by using rods or a pendulum. Dowsing is also used as a method of finding lost items, water, missing persons and spirits.

Ectoplasmic Mist is a misty, foggy cloud that appears in a photo where paranormal activity is occurring. It is believed to be the energy of a spirit. The mist is rarely seen at the time.

EMF Meter is a device that picks up electronic and magnetic fields. It is thought that spirits create distortions in the atmosphere that the Electro-Magnetic-Field Meter picks up.

Empathy is a form of telepathy where the empath is aware of and often feels, the emotional state of the spirit.

Entity is a term that refers to an intelligential energy who can communicate and make physical contact to the very sensitive.

ESP (Extrasensory Perception) is when a person has the ability to gather information about people, places or events, without the aid of any of the five human senses.

EVP (Electronic Voice Phenomenon) is a simple method in which you can pick up a spirit's voice by using a recording device. These spirit voices can also be captured on camcorders.

Exorcism is a ritual to remove detrimental or harmful spirits that have attached themselves to people or places. An Exorcism is performed by priests or demonologists.

Exorcist is a person that is skilled in the act to remove demons from another person or place that is possessed.

Family Apparition is a ghost that haunts one particular family. In some instances when the ghost appears it is an omen that someone in the family is going to die.

Ghosts are the souls of people or animals that have died but have not gone on into the light to complete their journey to the spirit world. They have remained on the Earth's plane and that's why they can be sensed more easily than spirits.

Ghost Lights are bright glowing orbs. They are most often seen in cemeteries floating over the graves. When you walk towards them they disappear or move to another spot.

Haunting is a place where reported, ghostly activity has taken place over and over for a period of time. This activity could be the results of an intelligent haunting, residual haunting, or poltergeist haunting.

Hypnogogic is someone who has had spirits invade their dreams in order to give you a message or warning.

Intelligent Haunting is when the entity invading the space is aware of you and present conditions. Often they try to communicate with the living.

Intuition is the act of knowing without the use of usual rational processes.

Based partly on subconscious pattern association of known information, and partly on subconscious psi impressions.

Malevolent is a term used to signify an entity that has ill intent towards the living.

Medium is a person that can see, hear or sense the dead and communicate with them.

NDE (Near Death Experience) is when a person dies for a short period of time before being revived and they can remember the experience of being separated from their earthly body. They often have recollections of being in a bright white light and may report seeing deceased loved ones. Many believe that once a person has a NDE, the veil between life and death is thinner. It's often been said that after such an experience, a person has one foot in life and the other in the afterlife.

Orbs are globe-shaped lights of energy caught on film, believed to represent the spirit of an individual that has died.

Oracle is a medium that can communicate with spirits to obtain information about the future. Oracles are recorded to have existed in the time of the ancient Greeks and Romans.

Ouija Board is a tool used to communicate with the spirit world. There are numbers, alphabet, and the words "yes", "no" and "good-bye" printed on the surface of the board. The persons using this device place their hands on a planchette that moves without aid while asking questions. As the planchette moves it will stop at the different letters to spell out the message. Extreme caution should be used when using a Ouija Board as the user has no control over what type of entity comes through.

Out Of Body Experience means to be able to leave your physical body and project your soul, consciousness or what appears to be your mind to another place and return via a silver cord.

Paranormal is any experience that happens beyond the range of scientific explanation or normal human capabilities.

Parapsychology is the study of apparent new means of communication, or interaction, between organisms and their environment (commonly referred to as psi, or psychic ability), beyond those presently understood by the scientific community.

Planchette is a triangular tool used as a pointer with the Ouija Board for purposes of receiving messages from spirits or ghosts.

Poltergeist is believed to be a noisy, mischievous spirit. It is suggested that many poltergeist focus on an individual in the household that is under some form of emotional stress. This type of ghostly activity include scratching, banging, objects disappearing and then reappearing, levitating, and in some cases fire.

Possession is when an evil entity takes over a human body. This allows the spirit to use the host by alternating his own will.

Precognition is to know about incidents or events before they occur.

Precognitive Dreams are when an individual dreams about events or incidents before they happen.

PSI is a general term for parapsychological phenomena that includes informational (RV, ESP) and energetic (PK) effects. Psi, or Y, is the 23rd letter of the Greek alphabet.

Psychic is a label used to denote a person who appears to be especially gifted with, PSI abilities.

Psychokinesis is the ability to move objects with the power coming from the mind. See Telekinesis.

Psychometry is when you touch an object with your hands for the purpose of getting information about the object, it's creator, its owner, or it's history.

Reiki is a specific form of energy healing, in which hands are placed just off the body or lightly touching the body, as in "laying on of hands" in order to heal.

Reincarnation is a belief that once a person dies his soul returns to a new body where it will continue its lessons about life and how to reach enlightenment. It is believed that numerous reincarnations may be necessary for the soul to learn and become closer to the goal of perfection.

Remote Viewing is the ability to access distant information through methods of visualization.

Residual Haunting is when the entity is unaware of the living. They do the same actions at the same time, on a loop, like a video recording repeating itself.

Scrying is a form of divination, which a person focuses on an object in order to see an image. This object could be a reflective surface such as a mirror, crystal ball, or a even smoke or a flame. The images that appear are often symbolic and give answers to a question. It is believed that a spirit usually generates these images.

Séance is where a group of people, sitting in a circle holding hands, attempt to contact the dead.

Sensitive refers to a person who can actively feel the presence of paranormal energy.

Smudging is a form of cleansing or clearing a spirit from an area by burning white sage and wafting the smoke to purify the area.

Spirit is a deceased person who has already gone into the light.

Spirit Guide is an ancient, wise spirit that guides the person it is assigned to. When in dire need this person may receive a premonition or intuition from the spirit guide, alerting them.

Spirit Photography is a photograph that contains a body, face, shadow, orb, mist, light anomaly or other unexplained forms believed to be that of a deceased person.

Synchronicity is meaningful coincidences, often mediated by subconscious psi activity. Our intuitive/psi faculty nudges our paths into meaningful intersections in times of need.

Supernatural is a term used when an unexplained occurrence takes place out of the realm of our understanding.

Table-tipping (Typology) is communication with the spirit world but by the use of a table. By laying hands on a small table and repeating "Table rise, table rise", a slight movement starts. The group instructs the table to tape once for yes and twice for no The table will tilt back and forth making a tapping sound in response to questions the group asks.

Telekinesis is where a person can move an object through the power of thought without physical means to move the object.

Telepathy is a method of thought transference including the sending and receiving of thoughts from one mind to another.

Teleportation happens when an object can be transported from one location to another by disappearing and then reappearing in a different place. They can even go through solid objects.

Vortex is believed to be a means of travel for the spirits, often in the orb form. It's believed that the Earth contains numerous natural Vortexes in various locations around the globe.

24

HAUNTED LOCATIONS

Enjoy hearing about my paranormal experiences? Create a few haunting memories of your own and maybe—just maybe—see a ghost or two for yourself. Be sure to give them my regards. Happy hunting!

Ashland
120 Sycamore Road
Lexington, Kentucky 40502
Phone: (859) 266-8581
http://henryclay.org

Benjamin Head House
11601 Main Street
Middletown, KY 40243

Boone Tavern
100 Main St. N
Berea, KY 40403
(800) 366-9358
www.boonetavernhotel.com

Buffalo Trace Distillery
113 Great Buffalo Trace
Frankfort, KY 40601
www.buffalotracedistillery.com

Conrad-Caldwell House Museum
1402 St. James Court
Louisville, KY 40208
www.conrad-caldwell.org

Farmington
3033 Bardstown Road
Louisville, KY 40205
(502) 452-9920

German Reformed Cemetery
10609 Watterson Trail
Jeffersontown, KY

Hayswood Hospital
4th Street
Maysville KY 41056

Locust Grove
561 Blankenbaker Lane
Louisville, KY 40207
(502) 897-9845
www.locustgrove.org

Long Run Cemetery
Old Stage Coach Road
Eastwood KY
(502) 241-1519

Middletown Historic Cemetery
Old Harrods Creek Road
Middletown KY 40243
(502) 245-2762

Middletown Toy Museum
11601 Main Street
Middletown, KY 40243

Mount Eden Cemetery
Highway 44 West
Shepherdsville, KY

Nunnlea House
1940 South Hurstbourne Parkway
Louisville, Kentucky 40220
(502) 267-8780
www.nunnlea.com

Octagon Hall
6040 Bowling Green Road
Franklin, KY
(270) 586-9343
www.octagonhall.com

Peewee Valley Confederate Cemetery
Maple Avenue
Peewee Valley, KY 40056
www.peweevalleycemetery.org

Tom Sawyer State Park
3000 Freys Hill Rd.
Louisville, KY 40241
(502) 429-7270
http://parks.ky.gov/parks/recreationparks/tom-sawyer

ABOUT THE AUTHOR

Terri Grimes is a multi-published author of Paranormal Romance. Information about her works can be found on the Internet at www.TerriGrimes.com

Made in the USA
Charleston, SC
18 March 2014